Tana Umaga

A Tribute to
a Rugby Legend

TANA UMAGA

A TRIBUTE TO
A RUGBY LEGEND

by John Matheson

THE COMEBACK KID

AFTER every test in 2006 Graham Henry would check his phone. If it hadn't arrived the All Blacks coach knew it wouldn't be far away. And as the team's winning run stretched through the Bledisloe Cup and Tri-nations championship he began to rely on the weekly text message from his former captain.

"He has texted me after every test match saying 'well done' and told me to pass the message onto the troops," says Henry. "He really cares about this team. He hasn't been involved since the end of 2005 but he is connected to us in a major way. His mere personality and presence has affected a lot of guys in this team and their ability to play the game. They all look up to him and use him as a role model, to strive to be the best you can be. Tana's had some challenges over his career, as a young player coming in, those development years and then on to becoming one of the great players and then as one of the great All Blacks captains.

"The players in the team look to him as an inspiration. Some are very close to him, particularly the Wellington boys because they're still rubbing shoulders with him from time to time. I've talked to Tana several times over the telephone over the last two or three months and I've got a huge amount of time for him. I really respect him as a person and he's still obviously very keen for the team to do well. And why wouldn't he be? In many ways this is his team. That's the impact the man has had on some of these players."

CERTAIN things just don't happen in sports. A hard court doesn't get laid down at Wimbledon, the Warriors don't dominate the NRL and a fighting fit Jonah Lomu most assuredly doesn't get stood down from the All Blacks.

It was 1999 and Lomu was the biggest name in rugby. When international scribes contacted the All Blacks' media liaison Jane Dent, Lomu was always at the top of priority interview requests. It didn't matter to them that he wasn't in John Hart's starting line-up. Maybe that shouldn't have been a surprise. After all, Lomu was to rugby what Michael Jordan was to basketball. What Diego Maradona was to soccer. And what Tiger Woods is to golf. He was the sport's face. The name that corporate giants adidas signed to a six-figure sponsorship deal. The name that was linked to lucrative multi-million dollar contracts to gridiron and league teams. The name that movie producers fought over for a cameo in a James Bond movie.

But for all of Lomu's undoubted attributes the fact remained that he couldn't break into the All Blacks starting line-up. And it wasn't down to anything he was or wasn't doing. It had everything to do with the dreadlocked winger whose form was simply irresistible. Tana Umaga had recreated himself and was keeping the biggest name in rugby on the sidelines.

"Jonah is a freak," Umaga said in 1999. "He can do things that I will never be able to do. Sometimes at training, I watch him. He's awesome. He's bigger than me, he's stronger than me and he's faster than me. There isn't anyone in the world who can do the things he can do. That's what makes Jonah unique. There is no one else like Jonah Lomu. There will never be anyone else like Jonah Lomu."

And yet there he was. The man who'd been a boy from the wrong side of the tracks. The man who only a year earlier, in 1998, seemed to have thrown away the chance given to him by then All Blacks coach John Hart in 1997. The man that had become the talking point of the All Blacks with the 1999 World Cup only

months away. A man who, when you study his background, had no right to expect success in life, let alone on the rugby fields of the world.

The Umaga family of Wainuiomata has long been an advertisement for rugby and family values. Falefasa and Tauese Umaga may have only been able to afford an ordinary life when they arrived in Wellington from Samoa in the 50s but what they gave their five children in the ensuing years was anything but ordinary. Theirs is the type of family that beats the odds. It didn't matter to them that they didn't speak English or understand the new culture that surrounded their every move. It didn't matter to them that they spent the majority of their time in Wainui apart as they headed to their respective jobs – Falefasa to the local car factory and Tauese to the hospital where she worked as a nurse. All that mattered was that they were giving their children the best possible start in life.

"If you want to know where Tana gets his character from, you only need to look at our parents," says Umaga's older sister Sina. "They did it the hard way. They sacrificed everything to come to New Zealand so that when they had children they could be sure that we'd get the best education and be given the best opportunities. When you have parents like that you can't help but be influenced by them. When you see them go to work every day, see them send money back to their families in Samoa and see them make time for all of us regardless of how busy they were, you start to understand what character is all about. If Tana hadn't had the chance to see those things, I'm not sure if he'd be an All Black."

The chances of Umaga wearing the All Blacks jersey again after a horror year in 1998 seemed slim. After breaking into the side and playing six tests in 1997, the Wellington and Hurricanes wing was very much on the outer. Banished to the confines of club rugby his future looked grim. Ahead of him in the line for an All Blacks wing spot were some impressive names – Jeff Wilson, Jonah Lomu, Joeli Vidiri...

"I wasn't feeling right after that season.
I knew I was carrying some unnecessary weight and
I asked myself if I was really as fit as I believed I was.
I knew I would find the answer if I was honest with myself.
I was a bit disappointed in what happened so I took it upon
myself to get into shape and try to make (1997) a good one."

"Tana had a choice," says Sina. "He could decide that he'd had the jersey and give up any thoughts of playing for the All Blacks again or he could decide that he wanted his spot back and start doing the things that he needed to do to make that happen. It would have surprised me if he'd given up. I would have supported him if he had because at the end of the day he's my brother – he doesn't need a black jersey to impress me – but I would have been surprised. We're not a family that gives up. We've gone through too much to take the easy way out of things.

"Everyone loves a winner. In 1997 when he first made the All Blacks everyone from his past was crawling out of the woodwork. Everyone wanted to know him. Everyone wanted to be his friend. But people like that only see the good side of being an All Black. They see the money, the car, the clothes and the travel. But those people weren't around when he was dropped. He found out who his real friends were. When that sort of thing happens, you are forced to grow up pretty quickly."

This was the first of the great comebacks of Umaga's career but only the first of many recreations. But this one was significant because he had been widely written off after losing his way after the 1997 season.

Born in Lower Hutt on 27 May 1973, Umaga was a product of Parkway College in Wainuiomata and while he played rugby at the school it was rugby league that was in his blood. "I started wearing a Canberra Raiders jersey and buying *Rugby League Week*," said Umaga.

"I was a great fan of Brent Todd and Bradley Clyde and I followed the big games avidly. I'll never forget the Manly/Canberra final of 1986…"

When a friend, Aaron, suggested they try out for the Wainui under-16 team, Umaga was dead keen. "Aaron gave up after one go, but I was hooked. Wainui was one of the strongest clubs in the country. I enjoyed the game."

He made quick progress through the league ranks winning Wellington call-ups for the under-16 and under-17 sides before Howie Tamati named him in the Junior Kiwis side in 1991. A year later Frank Endacott picked him for the JKs as well – this time alongside future Kiwi stars like Ruben Wiki, Joe Vagana and Gene Ngamu.

"He was a real talent, every bit as good as Ruben Wiki," said Endacott. "He was good on his feet, had balance and skills, and knew where the goal line was. And he was a tough defender. I knew he'd go a long way."

Umaga could have been locked into league in 1991. Along with Willie Poching and Brian Laumatia he signed with the Newcastle Knights but within two weeks all three were back in New Zealand. "It was a dream of mine to play professional sport," said Umaga "but we were just kids and I realised I wasn't ready for that life."

By 1993 his older brother Mike – a Manu Samoa representative – persuaded him to play rugby for the Petone club in 1993.

"Mike has always been my biggest supporter. When we were younger we used to work out at the local ground in Wainui. Mike would make me run along the touch line and try and score in the corner. He would start at the goalposts and try and stop me. He usually won. I don't think he would now though!"

As a youngster, Umaga watched British soccer on television. His idol was West Ham and England star Trevor Brooking, who was then nearing the end of his illustrious career. Umaga wanted to be like Brooking.

Then basketball and golf came along. Umaga tried them all and found none complicated. In fact he excelled at all the sports he tried. "As long as they are sports you can count me in. It runs in the family," he said.

Umaga's mum Tauesa, a dab hand at basketball, is a foundation member of the famous Wellington Pacific Island Church netball club. His sisters Janice and Sina played basketball for Wellington and Rachel plays volleyball.

Falefasa played cricket and rugby, and wrestled and boxed in his youth. But he always had a passion for rugby and that rubbed off on his sons.

"(Dad) never came out and said you should play rugby or whatever," said Umaga. "In his own quiet way he encouraged me towards rugby. I could read the message between the lines – absolutely, positively rugby."

Frank Walker, who would go on to coach Umaga for Wellington's NPC side, remembers the day Mike brought his younger brother to Petone – the club he was coaching in 1993. "(Tana) looked like something the cat dragged in," said Walker. "His brother had been promising to bring him along to Petone for some time, but Tana had preferred league. That first time I met him, he was wearing ear-bangers and scruffy jeans and looked totally unenthusiastic about playing rugby.

"A couple of us had a chat with him and said that wasn't the sort of attire we encouraged in the club. So he borrowed a white shirt and jacket and looked a lot more presentable the next week."

Admitting that it took a while "to sort Tana the person out" Walker said that the moment Umaga first received the ball in senior club rugby it was apparent he was something very special. "He brought tackling skills from league and every time he got the ball he achieved something. He could zip and zap and penetrate – it was obvious he was an extremely talented footballer. The problem was Tana himself – he always seemed tired and lacking in enthusiasm."

Walker though recommended Umaga to Wellington coach David Kirk in 1994 and he promptly selected him for the province – Tana on one wing and Mike on the other – and his form for club and province saw him win his first black jersey with a call up to the NZ Colts side. He quickly forged a name for himself with his electrifying pace and he finished his first three seasons in the Wellington NPC side as the province's top try-scorer as he switched between wing and fullback.

By 1996, and the arrival of professional rugby in the form of the Hurricanes and the Super 12, he was putting pressure on All Blacks coach John Hart. Jeff Wilson and Lomu were the incumbents and held their positions for the tour to South Africa – much to the displeasure of Walker who accused Hart of being bias against anyone from Wellington.

Umaga too was disappointed and contemplated playing for Manu Samoa. "Tana was keen to fly to Apia to try out for the national team," Walker said. "(In 1996) he asked me if I thought he should have a go for the Western Samoan team. Knowing the kid's ability, I advised him to aim at the All Blacks. 'Give it one more year.' I said. '1997 could be your year. If you don't make it then, you probably never will.'"

Walker suggested Umaga work on his fitness over the summer. And he did – but not because of Walker. The All Blacks selector Gordon Hunter had rung Umaga and told him that if he wanted to make advancements in the game he needed to put the work in.

It was a phone call that resonated with Umaga. "I'd been thinking about trying out for Western Samoa, but here was an All Blacks selector letting me know he was interested in me. That was all I needed really."

Umaga fronted for Hurricanes training in 1997, slimmed down and fighting fit. He'd hired a personal trainer and trained six days a week and not the one day-and-a-bit average of the past years after he'd ballooned to 108kgs. He'd shed eight kilos and set personal bests in all sprints, strength and endurance tests at the Hurricanes' camp in Palmerston North.

"I was stunned when the team was first announced.
Now it is slowly sinking in and I'm over the moon.
When I got into the reserves for the trial I was rapt
just to be close to the squad and sharing in the environment."

His improvement was the talking point of the weekend and coach Frank Oliver couldn't wait for him to get on to the field.

"I wasn't feeling right after that season," Umaga said of 1996. "I knew I was carrying some unnecessary weight and I asked myself if I was really as fit as I believed I was. I knew I would find the answer if I was honest with myself. I was a bit disappointed in what happened (in 1996) so I took it upon myself to get into shape and try to make (1997) a good one."

No one was more surprised at his transformation than Walker. "It was as if a bolt of lightning had struck him between seasons," he said. "The player who had all this natural talent, but who had never extended himself, was suddenly super fit for the first time in his life. It was great to see. He became a human dynamo."

Umaga had turned to trainer Glen Jenkins and his workouts were revamped. Jenkins whipped the wing into shape with plenty of explosive exercises, sprint work, drills, and weight training. "I wanted to do it for myself. I had to put in the time and sacrifice," said Umaga who'd seen his All Black ambitions disappearing. "What's held me back has been my fitness, which has never really been great at all because I'm not a great trainer," he told Wellington's *Evening Post* in 1997. "Last year I'd train once or twice a week. Since the NPC I've been training four times a week with my trainer and spend the other two days in the gym … I've really decided to give it a go."

The full-time aspect of being a professional sportsman was something that "clicked" after that telephone call from Hunter. "I'd always shirked my responsibilities, never been a good listener, never been prepared to extend myself. Now rugby was my livelihood. I was being paid to play so I decided my attitude should be professional too. I made a conscious effort to change myself, from diet and fitness to attitude."

The move paid off when Umaga got his chance in 1997 after illness to Lomu opened the door to an All Blacks call up and Umaga didn't disappoint. He earned his spot after a stellar Super 12 season where he helped the Hurricanes to the semi-final of the competition for the first time and where he finished with 12 tries – second only to the Brumbies' Joe Roff.

One of Wellington's greats, wing Bernie Fraser, was all for Umaga cracking the All Blacks side ahead of Glen Osborne. "The really good wingers can adjust slightly and still beat guys," Fraser said. "Tana does this and has got wonderful speed. He's like (former All Black wing) Stu Wilson in that regard and has become a superb finisher. It's all very well saying he's been given room and chances but he has to finish those off and that's what he's done."

And it wasn't just his physical attributes that impressed Fraser. Umaga's mental toughness was also superb. Said Fraser: "To be honest I thought he was washed up (in 1996). He had an average season and didn't impress me. I knew he had talent but he didn't use it. But he went away and shed about 10kgs and was determined to make it back. He's recaptured that zip and is firing. And he's got that real hunger to succeed. That tells me he could cut it with the All Blacks … no worries."

Surprisingly though Hart selected Eric Rush and James Kerr ahead of Umaga in the shadow test side with the Wellingtonian only picked on the bench. But he would be named in the run-on team to play Fiji at North Harbour stadium on a night when Taine Randell, Anton Oliver, Ofisa Tonu'u and Charlie Riechelmann also won their first caps for New Zealand – the most debutantes in a game since the second World XV test in 1992.

"I was stunned when the team was first announced. Now it is slowly sinking in and I'm over the moon," Umaga said at the time. "When I got into the reserves for the trial I was rapt just to be close to the squad and sharing in the environment."

Much of the publicity that zoned in on Umaga after his call up focused on his famed dreadlocks –

some European journalists decided to make a big deal of the All Blacks' "first dreadlocked player". Umaga played along telling them no one had told him to cut them off and "I'd be like Samson if I had to cut them off. I'd lose my strength."

Predictably the game was a one-sided one. All the All Blacks attack went to the right and to Wilson – the Otago wing picking up five tries. Christian Cullen grabbed a brace as well and Umaga made it onto the scoresheet with a well taken score in the 71-5 win. For Umaga though – the game itself was the easy part – trying to fit into his new surroundings much tougher.

"I was rooming with Jeff Wilson," says Umaga. "He said hello and tried to be really nice. I put my bags on the floor and because he was a senior player I had to wait for him to pick his bed. I sat on a chair and just waited for him to go and lie down on a bed.

"You tend to get around with people you know, so I found (Hurricanes teammate) Alama Ieremia and became his shadow. It was unbelievable (being in the All Blacks) because you watch these guys for years and you wake up at three o'clock in the morning with your father to watch them play…"

The complaints about Umaga being a suspect roommates were quick to surface.

"Apparently I make a bit of noise when I sleep. My wife has no problem with it. It worked out really well for me because for the last eight years of my career I always had my own room! I was dreading night time when I was rooming with Goldie that first time. He said 'I hope you don't snore because I'm a light sleeper.' I was tossing and turning, trying not to make any noise. When I woke up in the morning there were pillows and shoes all over the place and he was really grumpy. The next night he took off and slept in the physio's room. He didn't really talk to me too much after that! The next week I roomed with Frank Bunce so I just put my bags on the floor and went straight to the physio's room…"

Some of the shine was taken off his test debut

when the great Michael Jones was carried off the field after he ruptured the patella tendon in his left knee in a season ending injury. The injury was "really disappointing," Umaga said. "It was such an achievement for me just to play with the guy – even if it was only for half an hour. The injury put a blight on the game for me."

The Samoan connection is an obvious one and one that saw Umaga himself a target of the Pacific Islands team. "It was exciting to think that Samoa was keen to consider me playing for them but I was born and bred in New Zealand and it was only ever going to be the All Blacks for me. (My brother) always thought I could make the All Blacks. He had a word with me and told me to stick with it. He was convinced I would be making a big mistake by committing myself to Samoan rugby."

Umaga played with a blue t-shirt given to him by Mike under his All Blacks jersey. It was a tradition he would continue with for years. "That way," Umaga said, "it's like I am playing for the both of us." The t-shirt brought him good luck too with two tries following his second test – the 93-8 win against Argentina in Wellington – and another coming in the series' second test in Hamilton, won 62-10.

He could have had a hat trick at Athletic Park but passed the ball to Josh Kronfeld with the line beckoning on the end of a dazzling 70-metre run. "I actually had heard Justin Marshall calling to me earlier in the run and I felt pretty stink about not giving it to him. I think I could have made it but we scored anyway and that's what counts."

Umaga took the step up to the Tri-nations in his stride. It helped that the team's spine – hooker Sean Fitzpatrick, No 8 Zinzan Brooke, halfback Justin Marshall and fullback Christian Cullen – was the best in the business as wins were recorded against Australia 30-13 (Auckland), 33-18 (Melbourne) and 36-24 (Dunedin) and South Africa 35-32 (Johannesburg) and 55-35 (Auckland). Umaga got on the scoresheet for the last game against the Springboks after he'd missed the Melbourne game with a sternum injury.

Bad news came before the final test of the Tri-nations in Dunedin. Umaga was relegated to the reserves bench to make way for Glen Osborne. It was a surprise to many but Hart wanted to give Osborne another test start – perhaps a sign of loyalty to the wing that helped deliver the All Blacks' first series win on South African soil a year earlier.

At the time Hart said form did not play a part in the selection. "As I've said to Tana, I don't think he should have any doubt on where he stands with the panel – we've been delighted with what he's done. Tana's a great example, a graphic example of the professional environment and how a young man says … well, here's a chance for a new career and a new life. I think he's built himself superbly on and off the field. We're seeing a very, very good all-round kid developing. He's done himself proud."

Regardless of the reasons for that selection, the return of Lomu for the end of year tour to Ireland, Wales and England, coupled with a serious loss of focus and form, meant Umaga wouldn't wear the black jersey for another 14 months.

At the beginning of 1998 Umaga was a part of Hart's February camp at Wairakei and after a disappointing Super 12 was included in the shadow test team for the All Blacks trial – albeit as a reserve. A late Lomu injury elevated Umaga to the starting XV and it looked as though he would indeed be back in black.

But Umaga lost his personal duel with Osborne in the trial and paid the price with a call-up for

New Zealand 'A' instead of lining up with the All Blacks against England. Joeli Vidiri was pulled into the All Blacks squad to compete with Wilson and Lomu for the wing berths.

It had been an ordinary year. And it didn't get any better in the NPC when it seemed like Umaga was in cruise mode. Hurricanes assistant coach Graeme Taylor had seen enough and called an evaluation meeting with Umaga.

"It had to be an honest meeting," Taylor said. "That was the only way we were going to get anywhere. Tana agreed that he'd had a disappointing year. He hadn't committed himself that way he had the previous year and I think he knew that he'd let himself down. But I sensed that he was determined to put things right."

Umaga hired Wellington fitness trainer Graham Lowe who a year earlier had worked with Taine Randell and Jeff Wilson. "Motivation wasn't going to be a problem for me," Umaga said. "Missing out on the All Blacks was a real disappointment. The boys ended up having a pretty tough year but at least they were playing for the All Blacks. I had to have a real long look at myself. I had to decide if I wanted it badly enough to put the work in. There was never any doubt about it. I needed to be an All Black again.

"I didn't come out of the Super 12 feeling very confident. It's hard to shine when you can't get your hands on the ball. Things didn't go my way, I might have lacked that confidence and my attitude slipped a bit. So probably the whole thing's been good for me. My attitude wasn't the greatest during the All Black trial, but not making the squad was the kick I needed, I think. I had the meeting with the selectors, they told me why I wasn't selected, and I took that on board. I knew I had to knuckle down and get back into it."

During his time with his previous trainer the longest run Umaga went on in the summer of 1996 was 40 metres. Lowe changed that. To help build his aerobic base Umaga was running intervals of anywhere between 50 and 1500 metres. He was also a regular at the Hurricanes gym working out with Alama Ieremia and Filo Tiatia.

The results were immediate. Umaga's biggest problem in 1998 had been his inability to relax. He was uptight… he couldn't relax. The reason for that was largely because he knew he hadn't put the work in after the 1997 season. He was an All Black and he thought he'd made it. And the hard work stopped.

"It's a trap a lot of young players fall into," Taylor said. "When you work hard to get to the top there is a natural tendency to relax. You want to enjoy it. But you can't stop doing the things that got you there in the first place. It's like that old saying 'it's hard to get to the top but it's even harder to stay there'."

Umaga thrived under Lowe. When he eventually fronted for pre-season Super 12 training he impressed with his enthusiasm. He was fitter than he was when he was an All Black and his confidence was back.

"People like to say that Tana is laid back," said Lowe, now Graham Henry's All Blacks trainer. "In a way he is. He can have a real calming influence on the younger players and he doesn't tend to let things get to him too much. But just because he is laid back doesn't mean he doesn't have a real sharp focus as well. When he decided he wanted to commit himself to the training, he was like a machine. His whole attitude was focused on being the best player he could be. The drive that he showed came from within. The credit for fighting back must go only to him. Ok, I trained him, his coaches coached him, but Tana was the one who had to front up everyday and do the work. The success he's had doesn't surprise me at all. I could tell he was serious about making it back to the top. He was driven from within."

Umaga's sharp focus was there for all to see prior to the Super 12 kickoff as he dealt with a trifecta of unforeseen events that would have derailed many aspiring All Blacks. In November 1998 the Petone sevens rugby team, which won a tournament in

Singapore, was kicked off a Qantas flight from Sydney to Wellington because the airline said players were in a "drunken state". Umaga was the captain of the side and that allowed journalists of the day to reprint news of his 1994 conviction for head-butting a woman outside a Dunedin hotel in 1994. Umaga pleaded guilty to assaulting a woman after a National Provincial Championship loss to Otago. His counsel told the Wellington District Court Umaga did not remember the incident, which happened when he was intoxicated. The court was told the woman was head-butted on the nose and received superficial grazing and a chipped tooth. Umaga was remorseful and wrote apologising to the woman.

And then in February 1999 Umaga, Cullen and Norm Hewitt were spoken to by the NZRU after an alleged incident at a party. The story broken in the *Sunday News* signaled the beginning of a love-hate relationship for the media who he'd embraced in his younger days. "I'd paid my dues for those things; it really got to me. They brought up something from even two years before the Super 12 was thought of and I'll never forgive them for that."

Sandwiched between those two unsavoury incidents was the death of 1988 All Black Aaron Hopa in a diving accident. Umaga was one of 1800 mourners to pay their respects to 'Hops' and his family at the Hukanui Marae in Gordonton near Huntly.

And since he'd lost his place in the All Blacks side he also had to deal with a number of unsolicited calls from agents representing a number of local and overseas rugby and league clubs. But he spurned them all to re-sign with the NZRU.

Umaga's form was so electric in the Super 12 that he had plenty of time to put into practice a new "eagles swooping" arms-out celebration after each of his tries. It is, said Tana, not a team thing. "I thought I would try something new – it's my own little thing. You see Goldie [Jeff Wilson] doing his thing. I thought, why not me?"

Certainly the Hurricanes' stoic coach Frank Oliver wasn't complaining. He would normally have been turned off by the antics of some of the modern-day professionals, especially considering his past as one of the hardest All Blacks of them all. But he could do nothing but smile as Umaga returned to his best form and scored tries against the Bulls, Cats and Sharks. Oliver had hoped to play Umaga at centre but his form was too good to even consider moving him from the wing.

Says Taylor: "When Alama was out injured, there was a lot of talk around that Tana should be tried in the No 13 jersey. But we didn't go with that idea because we were convinced that Tana's form on the wing was going to be good enough to get him back into the All Blacks side."

And so it was. Umaga was named in Hart's squad for the opening test of 1999 against New Zealand 'A' along with Wilson, Lomu and Cullen. Talk had been rampant that Cullen would win one of the swing spots as he could swap positions with Wilson. That left Umaga and Lomu battling for the remaining place in the backline. The Comeback Kid v The Man. Work Rate v Brutal Power. David v Goliath.

AS the World Cup approached John Hart had something of a conundrum. The All Blacks coach needed to fit four world class players into three positions.

He had hoped that by moving Jeff Wilson to fullback the Otago flyer would have more room to express himself. Why he felt he had to take the world's best fullback Christian Cullen out of his comfort zone in a World Cup year is something only Hart knows. But he was a desperate man after his All Blacks had lost five consecutive tests in 1998. And, as the saying tells us, desperate times call for desperate measures.

In Hart's brave new world Cullen would take his place on the right wing and Jonah Lomu on the left. Tana Umaga would start the international series there but Hart was convinced by the time of the World Cup in October Lomu would be back to his best.

History proves that Hart was right on that count but he hadn't counted on the blistering form of Umaga.

The back three of Wilson, Umaga and Cullen combined for the seven games before the World Cup – six tests and the All Blacks trial between the national team and the 'A' team, a match that was given All Black match status. Cullen and Umaga grabbed two tries apiece in the first two games, shared five scores in the second test against the French in Wellington while Cullen grabbed another three in the two wins against the Springboks. Wilson too had impressed at fullback – scoring five tries in the seven outings.

"I see Tana as having been one of the most exciting players of the year," Hart told the *Dominion*'s Lindsay Knight. "He's on fire. With Christian Cullen and Jeff Wilson, he has brought a whole lot of energy to our game. The work rate we've been seeking is something which has been best epitomised by Tana."

Hart said that Lomu being used only as an impact player might have put more public pressure on Umaga. "But I can assure you Tana has not been under that sort of pressure from within the team."

Umaga admits to an awareness of that pressure and said that at the start of 1999 even he would not have contemplated being picked regularly ahead of Lomu. "I'm only human and I got a bit of a fright myself that I was being picked ahead of him, so the pressure was on from the start."

And although he relishes playing a full 80 minutes Umaga said he was content that generally he has been the one replaced when Lomu comes off the bench. "It's just being part of the game plan and they've got to put the big guy on at some stage. He really is the impact player. When he comes on you can see it in the opposition's eyes. They're feeling tired and now they've got to try and cater for him!"

Umaga's form meant Lomu was on the outer but Hart was determined Lomu – his not so secret weapon – be unleashed at the World Cup, the tournament he completely dominated four years earlier in South Africa. Hart solved the problem, or so he thought, by moving Cullen to centre and using the back three of Lomu, Umaga and Wilson. Cullen had scored two tries from centre in the 34-18 Tri-nations win in Pretoria when he moved to the midfield after Daryl Gibson was injured.

It was, of course, a fatal mistake. But that was to still play out over the next six weeks as the All Blacks headed for England on September 24. They were seen off by 2000 fans as they boarded a specially painted Air New Zealand plane adorned with an image of the All Blacks front row. Umaga was wearing a good luck charm giving to him by his Wellington captain Norm Hewitt on behalf of the Wellington City Council. Ieremia and Cullen where also given the Maori pendants carved from 100-year-old kauri wood taken from an old door frame from Athletic Park. Umaga's pendant was a miniature wahaika (digging tool); Ieremia's a patu (weapon) while Cullen, bizarrely, was presented with a kotiate – a tool used in circumcision.

In the tournament's first game Umaga was switched from the left wing to the right flank to make way for Lomu. And any talk it was just a trial for Lomu was put to bed when he scored two tries in the 45-9 win against Tonga at Bristol. With the next game against England there was no way Lomu would find himself back on the bench. He'd scored four tries against England in the 1995 World Cup semi-final and in the intervening years the Poms had shown no signs of healing the mental scars from that June day in Cape Town.

But it was Umaga – who had suffered a head knock against the high-tackling Tongans – who had the early impact at Twickenham as he threw a miracle ball to Jeff Wilson to score in the corner and give the All Blacks an early 10-0 lead. Lomu and Byron Kelleher would also grab tries as the All Blacks cruised to a 30-16 win.

The All Blacks juggernaut continued five days later when they overwhelmed Italy 101-3 at Huddersfield. Umaga sat out the game as Hart gave Glen Osborne a run at wing. But there was never any doubt Umaga would be back in the XV for the quarter-final against Scotland.

And before the match he backed Cullen and the controversial move to centre that had the talkback callers back in New Zealand up in arms. "It was a big move for Christian," said Umaga. "But he's fronting. You put him anywhere and he'd always give 100%. Everything comes with time. We're still getting used to the lines to run and places to be. But it's coming, everyone is trusting each other now. We still made a lot of errors against England and the challenge is to eliminate them. I think it's a matter of sticking to the basics and not getting too excited when the chances come. If you can stay calm and let the ball do the work, things will happen. And with the talent we have, if we can unleash things out wide, it's so exciting."

While the game against the Scots wasn't exciting the All Blacks got the job done with a 30-18 win. Much was made of the All Blacks' lineout woes but Umaga at least was back to his try-scoring best. His two tries were his first since a hat-trick against France at Athletic Park – a dry run of six tests. "I had a chance for a third but I had cramp in my leg when Christian Cullen made a break in the second half. I knew I couldn't run fast enough to go wide on the outside so I had to cut in and the chance was lost."

The All Blacks were now 4-7 favorites to win the Rugby World Cup with bookmakers William Hill. France, their semifinal opponents were sitting 16-1. The odds remained constant even after Hart dropped the bombshell of the tournament by opting for Kelleher to start at No 9 ahead of the experienced Justin Marshall. With Andrew Mehrtens bracketed with Tony Brown as he battled with a bruised knee there were plenty of flags raised for what was about to happen – but all of them went unnoticed by the masses.

And sure enough, in one of the biggest upsets in sporting history, France thumped the All Blacks 43-31 at Twickenham to set up a Cup final against Australia. At 24-10 up, six minutes into the second half, the All Blacks were cruising. Unfortunately, they couldn't get out of cruise mode and France put on an incredible 33 unanswered points before a consolation Jeff Wilson try in the dying seconds. New Zealand had the benefit of a 20-9 penalty count from Scottish referee Jim Fleming, but was out-tackled and out-thought by a passionate French team on its way to the greatest win in its rugby history. Never before had New Zealand let in 43 points in a test. Hart watched his team's lead slip from 14 to two, then slip further to a five-point deficit, before he made changes in the 17th minute of the second half. But the damage was done.

Umaga and Cullen ran into each other trying to take a high ball, Wilson and Umaga looked aimless when they managed to hold onto the ball and the forwards were miles off the pace in the mental and physical battle.

It was a dropped ball from Umaga that was kicked 70 metres by Oliver Magne for Philippe Bernat-Salles to just beat the covering Wilson to the touchdown. Game over. New Zealand's World Cup quest was in ruins.

"I was pretty much gutted by (the loss)," Umaga said. "What made it worse was I didn't play well. I made errors I hadn't made all year. Maybe I was trying too hard, I don't know what happened. I had a couple of sleepless nights after it. I'm pretty hard on myself,

"Jonah is a freak. He can do things that I will never be able to do.
Sometimes at training, I watch him. He's awesome.
He's bigger than me, he's stronger than me and he's faster than me.
There isn't anyone in the world who can do the things he can do.
That's what makes Jonah unique. There is no one else like Jonah
Lomu. There will never be anyone else like Jonah Lomu."

but you have to try and move on. It's something I won't get over for a long time. I'll be looking to take some positives out of what happened for the future."

Umaga said there were no signs that things were not right in the buildup to the French game, though he said the All Blacks "took the foot off" in being outplayed in the second half of their quarterfinal against Scotland. He said that at 25-3 at Murrayfield the players may have started thinking about their semifinal. Against France he said the players probably thought "we had it in the bag" when ahead 24-10, and they should have known better.

"At this level you can't think that way, and everything the French did came off," he said." We had been warned. We let our guard down. We knew what they were capable of. We showed inexperience and complacency. Maybe we underestimated them."

The misery wasn't over for Umaga. In the third and fourth place playoff against South Africa he was pulled off and replaced by Pita Alatini after fluffing a dreadful chip. Head sunk, he walked off Cardiff's Millennium Stadium muttering to himself. He made a vow that we would return to the rugby's biggest stage and right the injustice of the last five days.

REDEMPTION MAN

THERE have been plenty of times when he wished he could turn back the clock. But no more. It's not that he was a nonconformist or anything. It's just that in the past he wasn't ready to accept responsibility; it wasn't his karma, wasn't his culture. Now though, after a long, often difficult journey of discovery, New Zealand was witnessing the prime of Mr Tana Umaga.

THE reincarnated version of Tana Umaga wouldn't appear for another five months but the first signs that he meant business came within weeks of the Twickenham disaster. As he brushed off the aftermath, dealt with collateral damage and ran the stench of despair off his body from his and the All Blacks' failure at the World Cup, Umaga called a meeting with the new Hurricanes coach Graham Mourie. Umaga "enquired" about switching positions. He wanted to be a centre.

It had only been 17 days since the end of the All Blacks' World Cup but Umaga – never slow to sense an opening – floated the change from No 14 to No 13. With Christian Cullen destined to return to fullback and Alama Ieremia a more than capable No 12, Umaga could see a long term future in black in the midfield.

Mourie – the great All Blacks captain from the 70s – needed to be convinced. Ieremia was the leading candidate for the centre position with the Hurricanes while Jason O'Halloran and Paul Steinmetz were also capable of playing in the middle of the backline.

"I really think it is a matter of sitting down with Bryan Williams, who will be coaching the backs, and working through our options," Mourie said at the time. "It's fair to say we have a few options on our hands, and all are experienced players. It's a matter of working out our best mix and going through things once we get the squad together."

Three days after his meeting with Mourie, Umaga had a new Hurricanes teammate. Jonah Lomu had signed for Wellington and the prospect of the All Blacks back three many wanted to see at the World Cup – Cullen, Umaga and Lomu – excited franchise's bosses. Umaga still wanted to switch positions but the potential potency of the trio would prove too enticing for Mourie and Williams to ignore.

And with the way Umaga started the Super 12 it was hard not to side with the coaches. He grabbed four tries in the first two games of the tournament – one against the Sharks and three against the Reds – as the 'Canes went 2-0.

Umaga's season hit a road bump in the next match against the Highlanders at Carisbrook when he was sent off after he chopped down flying wing Romi Ropati. Referee Paddy O'Brien said it was head-high and Umaga was shown the red card. "I thought I was hard done by. It was a reflex action. I might have deserved the yellow card but I didn't deserve the red one."

Umaga was subsequently banned for one game. And, as if to prove a point, in his comeback game against the Cats he grabbed two more tries – his fifth and sixth in three games. It was the sort of form that had many salivating including the World Cup winning wing John Kirwan who declared Umaga the best all round player in the position in the world. "He's the most complete," the 63 test All Blacks said. "He's strong, fast, has a good step, has got the size and has a fantastic work rate which means he does so much off the ball and is never really out of the game. He's got good skills and has been on his game for the last two years."

Ironically after that high praise Umaga failed to touch down for the rest of the tournament. And as the tries dried up, the Hurricanes season went off the rails as they lost four of their last six games. But significantly Umaga's form, and work rate, was as good as ever and on April 29 he finally got his opportunity to don the No 13 jersey he craved. With O'Halloran suffering from concussion Umaga was moved to centre for the game against the Waratahs in Sydney.

The Hurricanes' backs coach, who played 10 of his 113 games for the All Blacks at centre, was confident his charge would make the transition to centre with ease. "He's got the skills to play there," Williams said at the time. "He is explosive, has good passing and handling skills and a high work rate. It's not easy to make the change but he's played a lot at centre in his early days and I think the way he generally plays the

"Things off the field have made me more mature as well, becoming a father for a second time. My family, my wife, getting married, that's made me grow up as well. Having that responsibility off the field has made it easier to accept that responsibility on it."

game is not unsuited to the centre role – high work rate, good handling and passing and good defence."

Williams said the main differences between centre and wing were the positional duties on defence. "As a winger you've got a role of being almost another fullback, whereas at centre you do a lot of running off the ball both on attack and defence. You're running decoys and frequently moving up and back without having to make tackles, so there are lots of positional requirements."

As it was Umaga thrived in the new role. He broke the line, set up his wings and made a number of bone-crunching tackles against the Waratahs backs in what, still to this day, is one of the gutsiest performances every produced by the Hurricanes. With Lomu sent off the 'Canes, with 14 men and sometimes with only 13 on the field, held on to win 27-20. Umaga's combination with Alama Ieremia, who played at second-five, was sublime and the prospect of them linking together in the All Blacks' backline was all of a sudden a massive talking point amongst the country's rugby commentators.

But any hype around the public airing of that argument was quelled when Umaga pulled out of the 'Canes' road trip to South Africa – and the team's last two games of the tournament against the Stormers and Northern Bulls – so he could be on hand for the birth of his second child Gabrielle.

When he addressed the press about his decision it was a sign of things to come. Umaga was no longer happy for others to make decisions for him. He was in charge and he let everyone know it.

"It's a decision (to stay for the birth) that I've made and the team's stuck by me," he told reporters. "I love the team and I would do anything for it, but my child will be around a bit longer than my rugby team will. It's something I don't want to miss, and the team fully understands. But there will be a part of me torn away with them. And I will be watching their every move. If we have the baby early, hopefully I can get on a plane

to South Africa and get over there if they still require me."

While his teammates were in South Africa, Umaga – who was now determined to play centre on a fulltime basis, began putting pressure on his employers. Backed by his manager Roberto Brady, Umaga dropped a bombshell when he confirmed he would consider moving to another province to enhance his chances of playing in the No 13 jersey and grabbing the All Blacks' centre role. "If I want to stay at the top level I think I have to move in (to centre)," he said. "My contract with Wellington comes up for renewal at the end of this year, so if an opportunity with another province came up I'd have to look at it."

It was a shrewd move. Within days new All Blacks coach Wayne Smith was saying he'd consider Umaga at No 13 while Wellington's bosses were frantically negotiating with Brady as they put a new and improved offer to the player. "We believe we can accommodate Tana and his intentions," Wellington Rugby Union CEO David White was quoted as saying.

Umaga went on to play in all seven tests in June through August as the All Blacks failed to wrestle the Bledisloe Cup or Tri-nations trophy from Australia's grasp. All of Umaga's games were on the wing as Pita Alatini and Ieremia filled the midfield roles. And his form was exactly where it was a year earlier – before the disappointment of the World Cup. He opened his international with a double against Tonga, grabbed four tries in the two tests against Scotland, another in the "game played in heaven" against Australia in

Sydney and scored twice in the loss against the Springboks in Johannesburg.

And all this despite one of the most testing times of his career.

After the All Blacks' 25-12 victory against the 'Boks in Christchurch, Umaga's life came crashing down around him as he found himself on the front pages of every newspaper in New Zealand. Umaga had been filmed in a drunken state wandering through central Christchurch. TV3 ran the video and All Blacks manager Andrew Martin was forced to admit that Umaga had had too much to drink and that he had been involved in a verbal exchange after he was insulted and had his dreadlocked hair pulled throughout the evening.

"Towards the end of the evening he was involved in an exchange of verbal insults," Martin said. "The cumulative effect of the earlier insults had made him a bit sensitive and he reacted angrily. There was no physical confrontation. Tana was subject to quite a considerable degree of abuse during the evening. His response and behaviour was entirely appropriate and he should be acknowledged for that. The other side of the coin is what we saw on the video which is the lack of sobriety. We all expect New Zealand men to go out and have a beer on the Saturday night after a game of football, and All Blacks are no different in that regard, but we have public responsibilities as All Blacks and role models. From that point of view it is quite unacceptable for an All Black to get as drunk as that in public. We are very disappointed and Tana is equally, if not more, disappointed."

Umaga stayed silent for two weeks. The day before the next test – against the Wallabies at Wellington – he broke his silence when he spoke to the *Evening Posts'* David Ogilvie. "It's not something I'm proud of – I'm quite embarrassed about the whole thing. And it's obviously opened my eyes to just how far we are 'up there' these days as far as the public is concerned. Every move we make is noted. It's always been that way, but for me it's got to the stage where I can't do anything."

Despite what happened Umaga denied he has a drink problem. "No, I haven't had problems with the drink in recent years. It's just one of those things that just got out of hand. It happened without me realising it. I'm not a heavy drinker. I don't feel I have a problem. It could come to the stage (of giving up alcohol) but I can't ever afford to be that drunk anyway, even though I was enjoying myself. The important thing to me is that I feel I let the team down with everything going so well. And this week I want to rectify this by going out and playing my guts out – and trying to put things right. I just have to take it on myself to remember who I am and whom I represent – and the traditions we are trying to uphold and make important."

While the test was lost by a last minute penalty to Wallaby skipper John Eales, Umaga showed remarkable resilience to produce one of his best test match performances – the highlight coming when he set up Christian Cullen for one of the great All Blacks tries. It started 40 metres out with a long throw which was tapped down by Ron Cribb. A long pass from Justin Marshall to Andrew Mehrtens, Alatini and Ieremia then saw Ieremia turn his back on the opposition as Josh Kronfeld and Kees Meeuws supported him on either side. Ieremia slipped the ball to the supporting and rapidly moving Mehrtens, who flipped it straight to Jonah Lomu coming in from the left. Lomu scissored with Umaga going back to the left, and a bemused Australian defence allowed Umaga to race clear and put Cullen away.

Umaga celebrated his fine form by signing on with the NZRU for another four years and his road to the No 13 jersey was made a lot easier when Ieremia signed on to play out his career in Japan. Umaga was all of sudden the No 1 contender for the position despite the aspirations of Daryl Gibson, Scott McLeod and O'Halloran.

But before he could compete for the jersey on the tour of France and Italy, Umaga had some unfinished business – a dinner date with his family. "It's something

I've always done. Me and my parents get together and have a bit of a prayer (before a tour)."

This dinner though was significant because it clashed with the New Zealand Rugby Awards gala where he won rugby's highest accolade, the K R Tremain Memorial Trophy for rugby personality of the year. His white hot form good enough to overcome any hangover from his sending off against the Highlanders and his late-night Christchurch indiscretions. And it was form good enough to win, for the first time, the All Blacks No 13 jersey in the two tests against France and the one-off game in Genoa against the Italians as Auckland's Doug Howlett took his place on the wing.

While Umaga's performances weren't great, Smith was finally convinced Umaga was a long term option at centre. "I think he's going to be fantastic," Smith said after the second French test. "He's got all the qualities. He very bright, he's big, fast, very good defensively and understands the game. He fits into the system there, which he failed to do at times when he was on the wing. He's really picked up the lines for the centre and he has also stepped into the leadership-type role."

Umaga's leadership skills had attracted interest from Mourie as well. The Hurricanes coach wanted Umaga to captain the team in the 2001 Super 12. And he did – but away from the public and press' knowledge. In a bizarre move the Hurricanes named Taranaki prop Gordon Slater skipper. But Slater was never the captain of the team. Umaga was the skipper in every sense but because he had a distrust of many sections of the media – *Sunday News* and TV3 had been blacklisted by the player – Slater carried the captain tag publicly to save Umaga from having to front the media on a day-to-day basis.

Umaga had attracted more bad publicity at the end of the 2000 end-of-year tour when an off-duty civilian police employee said Umaga attacked him at the Maddox nightclub in Genoa at 3.30 am. He said Umaga was drunk and had been bothering him and the woman with him. He had been hit a number of times in the face before other players stepped in and stopped the attack. But no charges were ever laid against Umaga and no internal discipline was taken against him either. Still, as far as Umaga was concerned, the publicity was another reason for him to be wary of the media.

Umaga thrived once the Super 12 started. He was the senior figure in the team and he was being picked at centre. While the Hurricanes were as unpredictable as ever, Umaga at least was putting in consistent – albeit not spectacular – performances as he played outside O'Halloran and then Steinmetz as the 'Canes limped to a ninth place finish. During the tournament he brought up his 100th first class try. "I don't remember too many of the tries, it's the ones that got away that stick in my mind," he said. "There was one against the Chiefs in Rotorua in 1996, and one against France (at Athletic Park in 1999). I really butchered that one. I only had the fullback to beat and he got me."

Umaga "came good" in the No 13 jersey in the 'Canes' shock 41-29 win against the Crusaders in Christchurch in round six of the competition. After he set up two tries in the win he told the *Dominion*; "When I went to South Africa (for rounds four and five) I focused on getting back to the basics and doing a centre's job. Defining my role of what a centre should do. From there, within that role, I'm trying to expand and see what I can produce."

Umaga said he decided in South Africa, where the Hurricanes played the Sharks and Cats, that he had to crawl before he walked, and walk before he ran.

"I tried to 'run' as soon as I came back (to rugby this year). Last year I thought I had the position down pat and I thought I would try and expand it before I'd even started. It just wasn't to be. I was doing too much and I was getting out of position."

Umaga's move to centre wasn't accepted universally. The former All Black Richard Loe was convinced he needed to return to the wing. "His main problem is that he isn't getting the opportunities to roam that he does on the wing," Loe wrote in his *Sunday News* column. "He's an incredibly dangerous wing because he has the ability to come at you unexpectedly from the blindside. Centres play a more contrived style of rugby. They have to feed their outsides and that is not the sort of work that Umaga likes. Don't get me wrong. Umaga is more than adequate at centre – in fact he's better than most. But it might be time to find someone else instead of wasting a very good wing. Surely there's someone in New Zealand with the ability to take his place at centre. His kicking has been found wanting and that won't surprise many people since there aren't many wings in the world who can kick."

And former Springbok coach Nick Mallet said: "At the moment, I feel he (Umaga) is more effective on the wing, where he is devastating, as opposed to centre where he is good, but not yet great."

The criticism leveled at Umaga though was nothing like what Lomu had to put up with. He was lambasted by spectators, talkback callers, journalists and commentators.

"Jonah Lomu looks like a cumbersome ox rather than a rampaging bull and should realise that his sole strength is his strength and should therefore run at opponents and attempt to retain possession, neither of which he is inclined to do at the moment," Mallet said.

It would transpire in the years to come that Lomu was suffering dreadfully as his kidney began to fail – ending in the big winger having a transplant in 2004.

"At the Hurricanes the players were starting to ask questions about why (Jonah Lomu) was still playing. It actually came to a head and he told our coach that he was still pretty crook. Everyone was giving him a bit of grief, including myself. Guys were asking questions. You felt garbage when everyone found out that he was ill. He was prepared to give his life for us. In the end it didn't come to that, but it just shows you what he's like."

But at the time of his on-field struggles his teammates – Umaga included – were guilty of sniping behind his back.

"You can't say enough about Jonah," Umaga said in 2006. "He's such a giving person. My opportunity (in 1997) arose because of his illness. I knew that it was only going to be a matter of time before he came back. I knew I would only have limited opportunities before he came back. He could never do enough for you, which is probably one of his weaknesses because he's always so busy giving. When his illness came back to what it is now, he wasn't telling anyone. At the Hurricanes the players were starting to ask questions about why he was still playing. He just wouldn't tell anyone. It actually came to a head and he told our coach that he was still pretty crook. Everyone was giving him a bit of grief, including myself. Guys were asking questions. You felt garbage when everyone found out that he was ill. He was prepared to give his life for us. In the end it didn't come to that, but it just shows you what he's like."

As well as the criticism of the on-field Umaga, the off-field barbs kept coming as well. When Jerry Collins was involved in a bust-up at a bar in the middle of the 2001 international campaign, it seemed like every story written on the incident ended with the line *Last year Tana Umaga was involved in fight in Italy.*

"Whenever someone gets in trouble I always get associated with it because of what has happened in the past," Umaga said. "I can't help that. I can only be the person that I am. I have a real willingness to play this game to the highest level. I have a love for the game. I think I would be selling myself and the game short if I didn't give everything to it. What has got me here is by trying week-in-week-out to do my best and commit myself to the jersey – whether it be Petone, Wellington, the Hurricanes or the All Blacks. That's what I want to be recognised for. That's what people should write about if they want to write about me. But, for whatever reason, my past keeps coming back. But, you

know what? That's okay because I know I can't change that.

"Some of the things I went through… they are just not issues for me. They are issues for other people. If you look at them individually they aren't big issues at all and I left them behind straight after they'd happened. I moved on. I am at the stage now where I can honestly say that I don't worry about what outsiders think of me. I am not going to pretend to be someone that I'm not.

"It took me a while to get to this stage… you know, not worrying about what my image is. It has taken a bit of soul-searching and a few mistakes. But, that's just life. My mistakes are public mistakes. If I wasn't an All Black, no one would care. The thing with mistakes is that you have got to learn from them. I've learnt that you don't get flustered about things that you can't control. Like the press – they are going to do what they do and write what they write because it's their job. All I can do is do what I can do. Control what I can control. I can control what happens to my family. I can control how I look after them. I can control how I can become a better person.

"My family is a great source of strength for me. The worst thing about the times when I have got into a bit of trouble is that it has hurt my family. Even now (in 2001) when my name is brought up when someone else does something, I can see that. It hurts my family more than me. It's frustrating because I am trying to improve myself and not make those mistakes again. But, yeah, (my family) is where the strength to deal with everything comes from. I am determined not to put my family through any hurt again."

Umaga's realism came though in an interview with the *Weekend Herald* a few weeks out of the international season. He told the Auckland newspaper he had stopped drinking to prevent a repeat of the 2000 incidents. He had struggled to make the decision. "I thought, why should I change my life for these people. You can think all you like that you have a private life, but in reality these people will do this to you…"

The off-field distraction though had no bearing on his form as he did enough to earn a call up to the All Blacks who were onto their second captain in two seasons after Anton Oliver replaced Todd Blackadder. Umaga was now seen as the No 1 centre and he would play in all seven of the domestic tests in 2001. Cullen was missing from fullback – now replaced by Canterbury's Leon MacDonald – but Umaga didn't miss a beat without his Hurricanes teammate as the backs averaged seven tries in their first three tests of the year against Samoa, Argentina and France.

Overall the All Blacks stepped up a notch from 2000 but again they fell at the final hurdle against the Australians. John Eales had kicked a last minute goal against them in Wellington the previous year and now it was Totai Kefu's turn to play the role of heartbreaker for the All Blacks. With no time left on the clock at Sydney's Stadium Australia, the All Blacks led 26-22 – the Tri-nations trophy and Bledisloe Cup seemingly heading back to the NZRU's Wellington HQ.

Umaga had added to his own legend by playing in the test in Sydney. His partner's brother Raymond Tuhaka, a 37-year-old father of three from Wainuiomata, died from a massive heart attack two days before the test. After spending a night grieving with his partner Rochelle, Umaga informed team management he would play. And the win, which was within the team's grasp, was going to be the perfect dedication.

But…

Kefu, the Australian No 8, had been making a lot of ground in the back half of the game exposing the defence of his opposite Ron Cribb. Umaga, sensing danger, knew that when the Wallabies won a late lineout, the ball would eventually be worked towards Kefu. He went across to Cribb and warned him. He then said to Cribb that he would take Kefu if Cribb wanted help. The North Harbour player turned down Umaga's

request and within a minute Cribb had dropped off the tackle, Kefu had scored and the game was over. Cribb would never wear the black jersey again.

The missed tackle would also cost Smith his job. The All Blacks coach was in tears following the game and questioned his desire for continuing in the job. That was enough for the suits at the NZRU who moved to replace him immediately with the former midweek All Black No 8, Chiefs coach John Mitchell.

Umaga would clash often with his new coach. Perhaps much of that stemmed from Umaga's loyalty to "Smithy" – the man that made him the "unofficial" All Blacks vice-captain behind Oliver. "It's a humbling experience, being given this kind of role, but I'm proud to get it and hopefully I can live up to it," he said at the time of his elevation. "I've really taken a personal step up with my leadership and I'm trying to help out with how the team's running. I feel I've got a bit to offer and it's great the selectors are willing to listen."

The whole of the rugby nation was listening in the days after the Sydney loss when Umaga told the *Sunday Star Times* that the Tri-nations had lost its appeal for many players. It was an extraordinarily brave statement from a man becoming more and more comfortable with the spotlight.

"We are playing each other too much at the moment with the Super 12 and the Tri-nations," he told Duncan Johnstone. "Maybe it's just losing its appeal to the public and the players. Everyone is familiar with each other, especially with all the contact in the Super 12. My preference would have been not to play the Tri-nations every year, maybe once every two years, maybe even three years. We need different teams coming in. They are talking about having one window with the north and the south for international rugby and you could have a lot of good games there if they can get it right. We need a bit more value on some of the games."

Umaga would also take a swipe at the Super 12 saying it should be scrapped so players could focus on

club and provincial rugby. "It happens too early (in the year) for us and every year they seem to want to start earlier. I would rather push the Super 12 out and just have club rugby, the internationals and the NPC. It's the way it used to be but there are not many of us traditionalists left."

Umaga conceded the Super 12 had lifted the standard of rugby in New Zealand, but only for the elite players. "It's not the standard of the Super 12 I'm against, it's the timing. It's great rugby and I enjoy playing it because you get to travel a lot and play against the best players in the top three countries in the world. There's just too much of it. It's going to come to a stage where they (rugby administrators) have to be honest about it and admit there is just too much rugby. We are helping other countries become stronger by playing against them all the time."

The comments – while controversial – showed leadership. And so did what he said the day after the Sydney loss when he said the time for the All Blacks being the nearly men of rugby needed to come to an end. Quickly. "We're getting there, but we can only be getting there for so long. I would like to think that this is the last time we can say 'we're getting there', because we've used it before and we've used it too often. It's do or die now, and a lot of guys are feeling the crunch. Coaches and some of us players are starting to wonder whether it was ever meant to be. Maybe it's time for some of the personnel to change – maybe something needs to change."

Wellington's NPC coach Dave Rennie was convinced of Umaga's leadership ability and promptly offered him the captaincy of his province.

"Some people may have thought it was a strange decision given Tana's off-field problems," Rennie said, "but it was a very easy and clear-cut decision for me. I don't think Tana had major issues off the field. That Christchurch incident… the media that reported on it ought to look at themselves. There would have been a few of them that were in worse condition that night than Tana. The incident was blown all out of proportion.

"Wellington needed a leader. Tana was an All Black and we felt there was a certain amount of responsibility to go with that. For some All Blacks it's quite nice for them to sneak back into NPC rugby and just worry about their own game. But we needed more from Tana and he was the ideal choice to captain the side because leading is easy for him. There are a lot of people who talk it up and don't produce the goods on the field… Tana very much backs up what he says."

Umaga took 24 hours to think over the offer before accepting it.

"It was a surprise when he offered it to me," Umaga said. "I was wondering if I really wanted it… if I had it in me to do it. In the end I took it because of what Wayne Smith and (assistant coach) Tony Gilbert did for me. When they gave me more of a leadership role within the All Blacks it gave me a lot of confidence. Being asked to lead… it was a big thing. I hadn't really had to do that before. I learnt a lot from them as well as playing under Anton. I learnt that leadership was about honesty and being myself. The Wellington guys… I think they know I am genuine. They realise I'll go out there and play my heart out for the team. They know I won't ask anything of them that I'm not doing myself."

That Umaga thrived with the Wellington captaincy was a surprise to no one. Although he admitted at the time that a year earlier he is sure he wouldn't have even been considered for the job.

"I was the typical Polynesian. Very quiet. Generally Polynesians don't like confrontation when you are one-on-one with someone. Usually they'll keep the idea to themselves and concentrate on themselves. I was like that. I have come out of my shell this year. If you ask coaches from last year they'll tell you that I really did concentrate only on my game. I used to think that for me to give anything to the team I had to be 100 per cent focused on myself. I had to concentrate on getting my job right. Even if we lost, I was okay as long as I knew I had given everything I could. Now it's different. Now that I have an overall influence on everyone, it's more about the team. Maybe it's because I am Polynesian but, as a rule, we don't like telling people what to do. Even though I am the captain, I still don't tell people what to do. I'll just make suggestions. I'm lucky that the team supported me. They made my job pretty easy."

Umaga impressed all with Rennie and Mourie both suggesting he should be a serious contender for the All Blacks job under Mitchell. Mitchell though would retain Oliver in the job but Umaga's "unofficial" vice-captaincy was now official. Both he and Canterbury flanker Scott Robertson were named as Oliver's seconds-in-command.

"It's a great story isn't it," his former coach Smith said of Umaga's rise from the ashes of the controversies from 2000. "He got himself into a bit of trouble in the past but he's come through it. And the great thing is, he's done it himself. No one else can take credit for it. He has shown the ability to be hard, work at something he cares deeply about and not be swayed from it. It's something worth admiring."

Smith had planned to give Umaga more of a leadership role when Blackadder was the captain but said the Wellingtonian wasn't ready. Speaking in 2001 he said: "Before you can ask a player for leadership he has to command his position. There were things he had to work on to become a great centre. First and foremost it was about being a more disciplined defensive player. Centre is a real key hard-man role in the backline… almost like the loose forward of the

backs. He needed to be able to do his job in a disciplined way on defence before he could lead the outside backs.

"It was the same on attack. We had to do a bit of work on what he should be looking for out there. We worked on his ability to put others into space rather than being the penetrator as he was when he played on the wing. We wanted him to look for the mismatches, see where slow players were and be selfless. It was a matter of getting those two things sorted and then knowing that once he'd done that he would, at the very least, be leading by example."

Once that progress was made in 2000 Smith put into action the plan for Umaga to offer real leadership to the All Blacks.

"I saw some attributes in him that proved to me he was a leader. Firstly, he cares really deeply about the team, the black jersey and the results. Secondly, he is very uncomplicated and very direct. He is one of the few players who can tell his peers the way it is without fudging anything. He's quite hard in his own way. He can lay down the law and players will listen.

"He still had some areas to work on. When he knows that things aren't going right with the game plan, he needs to be authoritive enough to make the changes then and there. That's something he was trying to improve on. And he worked really hard at building relationships with the people around him – like the first five eighth, halfback and captain.

"I think he found that as he got more into it and got more involved with being one of the leaders the whole thing has meant more to him. I think in the past he tended to – when the game was over – be one of the boys. He is a lot more reflective these days. I think when things go wrong on the field it probably hurts him more, too."

Smith said that hurt was behind Umaga's "enough is enough" quotes after the Sydney loss. "He had something to say and he said it," said Smith. "I agreed with everything he said."

Umaga had no regrets about making the statement. "I said what needed to be said. I had to. You have to remember that at the time I was very low. The All Blacks have such a proud tradition and at different times we didn't reach those standards. I was trying to make the point that we need to be accountable as players. We can't keep trotting out the line about 'we're getting there'. We need *to get there*. We need to remember that each one of us is only a minder of the jersey we are wearing. None of us own the All Blacks jersey. We need to earn it. And the only way we can do that is by performing in it. By winning in it. The time for excuses is over. If some of us as players aren't up to the challenge then we shouldn't be in the team. I know that I wouldn't want to be in the team if I wasn't worthy."

Greatness, it is said, doesn't always arrive with a flourish. Sometimes it grows quietly, revealing itself gradually to even those with the best view.

"He has always been the quiet achiever," said Ieremia who played the role of Wellington, Hurricanes and then All Blacks mentor to Umaga between 1994 and 2000. "He went about his preparations for games on his own. He never said much. But with Tana, you always knew that if he was given a challenge, he'd put his heart and soul into it.

"People always like to talk about character. Part of Tana's character has been built from the fact that he has made mistakes. He can't escape the past… he knows that. It will be like a rock around his neck… he knows that. But I firmly believe that he will be judged ultimately in a good light because he has turned his wrongs into rights. He has had it hard. He has become a better person. Isn't that what we want from our role models?"

The 2001 end-of-year tour was significant not only because it was Mitchell's first but also because the first test of the tour, against Ireland, was the first for Richie McCaw – a player who would go on to forge a career that has him standing on the precipice of being one of the great, if not the greatest, of all of the All Blacks. The

tour also marked the beginning of the end of the All Blacks road for manager Andrew Martin – one of Umaga's greatest supporters through his problems in 2000.

But the results gave New Zealand rugby fans great hope as the Mitchell era began. Ireland were thumped 40-29 in Dublin, the Scots succumbed 37-6 at Murrayfield and a 77th minute try by Robertson secured a last-gasp 24-20 victory against the Pumas in Buenos Aires.

IT was a set up. Designed to end the immediate All Blacks aspirations of Tana Umaga and Taine Randell. But it was a set-up that backfired.

With a Super 12 between his first act as All Blacks coach and the next, John Mitchell was determined to make the All Blacks *his* team. He'd set a line in the sand when with little time between his appointment and the tour to Ireland, Scotland and Argentina, he axed three 'name players' – Jeff Wilson, Christian Cullen and Randell.

An injured Cullen, it transpired, had pulled out of the tour 48 hours before Mitchell named the team and told a press conference the champion fullback had been dropped because of a "loss of form". It was an embarrassing start to his reign but the point was made – Mitchell was going to shake things up.

And the two players immediately on his radar for All Blacks oblivion a year out from the 2003 World Cup were Umaga and Randell.

Umaga had started the year highly motivated. Mitchell had played him in all three of the 2001 tour tests and he was determined to maintain his standards into the new year. So much so that a Hurricanes management committee of physio Glenn Muirhead, doctor Dave Velvin and coaches Graham Mourie and Dave Rennie had to hold him back from January training with the franchise as they monitored his troublesome Achilles tendons.

He probably wished he wasn't fit when the Hurricanes opened their season with a record 60-7 loss to the Blues in Wellington. The result set the scene for another disappointing season as the 'Canes would end the tournament in ninth place.

Despite the depression of Hurricanes fans, Umaga enjoyed the majority of the season. "I am really enjoying my rugby now that I have picked up on the centre's game," Umaga said at the time. "There are still things to work on but I am far more confident than I was last year and at the end of 1999. It takes time to adjust to any position and I didn't want to just be a conventional centre, though I need to be at times and am forever working on my skills. It is important to recognise the space for the outsides; to put them away to score tries, because in the modern game, with defences so well organised, it is hard to score from set plays."

Umaga's enjoyment shone through with his performances. While many of his teammates were battling for form and confidence, Umaga was impressing. Jim Kayes, the *Dominion's* rugby writer said in May that Umaga was "a certainty" for All Black selection.

And when 2002 All Blacks skipper Anton Oliver received a year-ending injury in the second-to-last round of the Super 12 some astute rugby judges were backing Umaga to take over.

Former All Black captain Mourie said Umaga was up to the task. "He's shown a lot of ability in that area and I'm pretty sure he could do it," Mourie said when told of Oliver's injury. "Last year (Tana) took more and more responsibility with both the All Blacks and Wellington as a leader and he made a lot of sacrifices both on and off the field. He puts the team first always, which is important in a captain."

Stu Wilson – the one-time All Blacks record try-scorer was another supporter. Writing in his weekly column in the *New Zealand Truth* he said: "Looking for a leader? Thinking about getting the right man to take over the All Blacks? Then look no further than Tana Umaga. I've taken great interest in the captaincy debate following Anton Oliver's season-ending injury last weekend. And while many pundits are picking either Taine Randell or Reuben Thorne, I'd prefer Umaga. Certainly. My logic is based on the fact that Tana will be a certainty to start in every test. And you can't say that about either Randell or Thorne. I also don't agree that Umaga won't be able to do the job because he's "too far out" at centre. That's ridiculous. We hear so much about shared leadership anyway that the pack will have proven players of the the caliber of Randell or Thorne and Mark Hammett fulfilling a captaincy role. Umaga offers a range of skills to the All Blacks. I've already mentioned his credentials as one of the best centres around. He's also matured a helluva lot as a bloke in the past couple of years and that's seen him become a respected player on and off the field. He's now something of battle-hardened veteran of 37 tests and knows the workings of the All Black team and the historical significance and responsibility that goes with the black jersey. Sure, it's been a roller coaster ride for him but he's the sort of bloke who knows what it's like to fight back after being kicked in the guts. I also believe Umaga would be a more up-front and proactive captain than Oliver who seemed, at times, to be visibly weighed down by the job. The Hurricanes centre is also a player who would be inspired leading the All Blacks and in the process he'd lift the players around him."

And Chris Laidlaw, an All Black between 1963 and 1970 turned Sky TV commentator was another in the Umaga camp. "Teams invariably succeed when just about everybody is their own leader and when everybody takes full responsibility for getting his job done. When that happens captaincy is almost redundant. Players win matches as a result of their own

natural talent, their personal ability to concentrate on the job and their combinations on the field. It follows therefore that the issue of a temporary appointee to fill in for Anton Oliver is not something to wring hands over. Any one of three or four All Blacks could take it on but the main requirement is permanency of tenure in the team. In this regard Taine Randell is marginal. So is Justin Marshall. Some might say Reuben Thorne is too. Of the sure bets the strongest personality by far is Tana Umaga and nobody could say that he wasn't ready and qualified for the job. I'd give it to him in the meantime."

Umaga wasn't talking captaincy but he was, justifiably, confident of his involvement in the All Blacks set up. Towards the end of the Super 12, when he was struggling with an injury he was talking as though he was in the know. He wasn't… "I'll be out for two to three weeks, but that's when the Super 12 finishes so there should be enough time before the first test (in Hamilton on June 8)," Umaga said. "I don't think I'll lose too much fitness. It (the test) will be my first match since the Crusaders, but my match fitness should be okay after all the games I've played this year."

When Mitchell and his assistant coach Robbie Deans named their squad for the tests against Italy, Ireland, Fiji and Tri-nations, the writing was very much on the wall for Umaga. Mark Robinson, the Canterbury and Crusaders star, was a favourite of his provincial coach Deans and was seen by him as the No 1 centre. His two tries in the Crusaders' semi-final win against the Highlanders convincing Deans of his ability to perform on the world's biggest stage – test rugby.

Ben Blair, Roger Randle, Nathan Mauger, Pita Alatini, halfback Mark Robinson, Paul Miller, Jerry Collins, Greg Feek and Jason Spice were all dropped to make way for 15 Crusaders named in the 26 man squad as Deans flexed his selectorial muscle.

Sure enough, when the first test team of the year was named Umaga's name was missing. There had been much talk about him carrying a knee injury in the

build up to the test against Italy in Hamilton but interestingly the day Mark Robinson played in only his second All Blacks test, Umaga was in Wellington playing for Petone in a losing effort against Poneke.

A blow to Robinson's head against Italy made Umaga's return to the test side a formality for the team for the second test of the year against Ireland in Dunedin – one of ten changes as New Zealand rugby fans were introduced to "rotation" for the first time. Umaga and Howlett were the only non-Crusaders in the starting line-up. The test would be won unconvincingly and the team booed from field after the unimaginative and unspectacular 15-6 victory. Umaga, too, would have felt depressed after being hauled off in the 56th minute and replaced by the Crusaders' Daryl Gibson.

When it came time to name the team for the second Irish test in Auckland Robinson was back to full fitness. He was named in the 22 for Eden Park and Umaga, along with Randell (who was replaced by Simon Maling), was dropped.

Both players were told to play for a NZ Barbarians team against NZ Maori the night before the test. And both players were fuming. Randell, a former NZ Maori captain, was angry that he was being asked to play against the Maori side while Umaga – who had made it clear he was a centre first, second and third – was told to play on the wing.

"We were both involved against Ireland the week before and we got sacked off to play for the Babas," recounts Randell. "I wasn't happy about playing against

the NZ Maori team and said I'd rather go and play club rugby than play against them, or play for the Maori team. Tana too was frustrated. Playing for the Babas, on the wing no less, was the last place he wanted to be."

Randell and Umaga were left to devise a basic game plan to take on a Maori team that had been together for a while. And with the odds stacked against them the Barbarians convincingly came out on top 37-22 with both "former" All Blacks in inspirational form.

Umaga's pace – shackled at centre – surprised many and his work rate was literally second to none. He'd proved a point. The rugby nation had been shocked by his omission from the All Blacks and he paid back that faith with a stellar performance. But despite his form, the door to the All Blacks XV was still slammed shut.

Fourteen Crusaders were in the starting line-up for the test the following night – Jonah Lomu on the left wing the only non Cantabrian in the line-up that would defeat the Irish 40-8.

Umaga was given a token test call-up for the one-off test against Fiji. "It's been a psychological rollercoaster really, up and down, and up and down, but I suppose that's what they (Mitchell and Deans) want," Umaga said after the team was named. "I'm a bit of an old head now and I don't think it was a form thing. They wanted to give me game time and you just can't let self-doubt creep in. I felt I wasn't doing anything wrong and that I was still playing well."

Umaga would only last 21 minutes in the test before injuring his knee. But he was fit and available for selection before the Bledisloe Cup test against Australia in Christchurch two weeks later. But he was dropped from the 22 in favour of Gibson. Mitchell claimed they couldn't select Umaga because he had missed some training sessions – his 39 test experience apparently counting for nothing. He would instead turn out for Petone again.

"While we are usually pleased to have Tana back, this time it's the most displeased we have been – we'd much more like to see him in a black jersey today than a blue and white one," Petone coach Dion Ross said before the 20-12 loss to Oriental-Rongotai. "He's come back so many times and gifted us his game. Now it almost seems odd that he's there – so it's our turn to try and help him. It's the first time we've really had the chance to help him. We sympathise with the position he's in. And we're rapt to have him as always."

If Umaga was feeling the love from his club it certainly wasn't being replicated by Mitchell. After the Wallabies had been dispatched 12-6 Umaga was back in the squad for Gibson but was again named on the bench for the test against the Springboks behind Robertson. He was though feeling the love, if unconventionally from the country.

There was mass distrust in the Canterbury domination of the All Blacks. Some argued that Deans had too much say while others like Laidlaw – a former race relations conciliator – suggested something was amiss because the team was All White…

"One of the barely noticed features of last week's winning All Black team was the fact that it was as Pakeha in complexion as New Zealand has possibly ever fielded," Laidlaw wrote in the *Dominion*. "Setting aside a very tenuous Maori connection or two this was essentially the All-Whites dressed in black. The natural response to an observation like this is so what? Conventional wisdom has it that we don't talk about this any more, not just because it is a symptom of political incorrectness to do so, but because it simply has no relevance any more when it comes to our national sport. Or so we convince ourselves. However, it is a very interesting issue in the context of what John Mitchell considers to be the right kind of team to beat the likes of Australia and South Africa. The fact that Mitchell and Deans have opted overwhelmingly for a Pakeha squad might be an accident and it might not. I think not. Mitchell is a conservative when it comes to preparing horses for courses. He has shown that he values accuracy, consistency and reliability above flair

"Being asked to lead... it was a big thing. I hadn't really had to do that before. I learnt a lot from them as well as playing under Anton. I learnt that leadership was about honesty and being myself. The Wellington guys... I think they know I am genuine. They realise I'll go out there and play my heart out for the team. They know I won't ask anything of them that I'm not doing myself."

and imagination and, whatever one might think about the entertainment merits of this, he has proved his point thus far. It so happens that in his quest for these qualities he has opted almost exclusively for Pakeha players.

"There were howls of dismay earlier this year when he discarded players of Polynesian origin such as Pita Alatini and Jerry Collins from consideration. They were, in his view, simply not accurate or consistent enough and their tearaway tendencies were considered to be a liability rather than an asset.

"There was mystification in some quarters when Maori wings Roger Randle and Bruce Reihana were ignored for much the same reason. Neither can get through a full 80 minutes without committing at least one undisciplined howler. One howler might go more or less unnoticed in Super 12 but against the Wallabies it tends to lose you the match. Various Fijian and Samoan three quarters were flagged away for precisely the same reason.

"And then of course we have the case of the two highest profile Pacificos – Jonah Lomu and Tana Umaga. When these two were left out of the squad to take on Australia, people began to wonder if some kind of Polynesian purge wasn't under way."

Mitchell dismissed the claim. "There are 11 players in our squad of 26 that are non-European," Mitchell said in response to the offending article. "It's the last thing that even crosses my mind. I don't think about colour in any form of selection. I don't think conservatism is a word that I would use. I'm very interested in character. Character's probably one of the first pieces of criteria that I look at over and above rugby skills."

Former All Black centre Frank Bunce, who is Samoan and Niuean, was on the All Black tour to Britain with Mitchell in 1993. He said there was "no way" the former Waikato skipper was racist. "Knowing Mitch and Robbie Deans, and the people involved in selecting the All Blacks, there is no way you could brand them or their selection policy as racist."

But Bunce supported Laidlaw's suggestion that players of different races had varying strengths in their play.

"People won't like to hear this, but in some positions you need a bloke who will just put his head down all day and do the hard work. More often than not, that guy is white. The brown guy, the Maori or Pacific Islander, he likes the free-flowing game, he likes to roam in the wide open spaces. It's the nature of the people, it's not a racist thing."

That Laidlaw chose to write such a controversial article was largely down to the inconceivable omission of Umaga. Few rugby insiders could understand what was happening. Misinformation and distrust was the order of the day.

As it was Umaga would only have to wait 30 minutes before being called into action against the 'Boks. Robinson left the field suffering from concussion and Umaga had his chance. With Umaga outside Aaron Mauger he made an immediate impact as the backline at last found its fluidity. Four tries later the All Blacks had cruised to a 41-20 victory.

With Robinson ruled out for the rest of the Tri-nations Umaga had a virtual green light to start the final two tests against Australia in Sydney and South Africa in Durban. But his excitement was tempered with news from Mitchell and Deans that his natural attacking game was to be shelved. He needed to be more "structured" – a bit more like Robinson…

"Before I've been able to do just about whatever I wanted, mainly out of necessity because of the teams I was playing in," Umaga said. "But I don't have that

(roving commission) any more. That can be good because what you want as a player is to do your job and concentrate on just that. Robbie had told me to stay calm but I guess I was over-excited."

He admitted he was struggling with the demands of a more structured game, but was adamant he would change if that was what it took to stay in the All Blacks. "I don't think you will ever see me stop (popping up anywhere on the field). It's a part of me and it's a part of me I'm loathed to lose. I can't help myself at times but maybe you will see less of it. I'm still playing good footy and if I can fit into this regime I will be there. I want to be an All Black. If that means changing, I'll change."

The All Blacks lost in Sydney in another tight affair – 16-14 thanks to last minute Matthew Burke penalty – and held on to win 30-23 in Durban. The Tri-nations title was secured when the Wallabies lost to the 'Boks a week later 33-31.

Despite his limited playing time through the domestic series – and in another example of the curiousness the rest of the rugby world looked at Robinson's elevation ahead of Umaga by the All Blacks coaching staff – the Wellington skipper was named in a Tri-nations XV based on Zurich world player rankings alongside Werner Greeff (South Africa), Breyton Paulse (South Africa), Stirling Mortlock (Australia), Mauger (New Zealand), Andrew Mehrtens (New Zealand), Justin Marshall (New Zealand), Scott Robertson (New Zealand), Joe Van Niekerk (South Africa), Nathan Sharpe (Australia), Simon Maling (New Zealand), Owen Finegan (Australia), Greg Somerville (New Zealand), Jeremy Paul (Australia) and Bill Young (Australia).

Umaga was back in the news during the NPC a month later when eight weeks before the All Blacks were to tour England, France and Wales it was announced that skipper Reuben Throne would be stood down for the rest of the year. There was another groundswell for Umaga to be given the All Blacks captaincy.

Laidlaw saw an opportunity for Mitchell and Deans to make both a rugby and political statement.

"… Umaga is the logical candidate to replace Thorne. He is a dominating personality whose leadership has come with experience and confidence built up over a lengthy career at the top. He has become a successful provincial captain and will unquestionably be the captain of the Hurricanes next year, a job which 20:20 hindsight suggests he should have been given several years ago. He is, de facto, the leader of the All Black backline whenever he plays.

"Nobody would question the proposition that Umaga leads by example. His phenomenal energy, reflected in his workrate around the field, has become legendary and there probably isn't another player in world rugby, with the possible exception of Ireland's Keith Wood, who is so constantly and decisively involved throughout a game. Umaga is a roamer. He turns up all over the place. He is often seen in and around rucks and mauls when another body is urgently needed.

"And, by appointing Umaga as the captain, however temporarily, New Zealand rugby would send a definite signal about the hugely positive multi-culturalism of our game. Some would say this is irrelevant, that we are blind to such issues as race in the All Blacks and that it is wrong or embarrassing to highlight such things. That isn't the point. The importance of role models such as Umaga should never be understated, least of all by the premier sports team. A Samoan New Zealander as All Black captain would send an exceptionally positive signal."

Stu Wilson was a little more basic in his affirmation of Umaga. "It's obvious who should lead the All Blacks while Anton Oliver and Reuben Thorne recover from injury. In fact I'm amazed that one of our most experienced players and genuine leaders hasn't been mentioned in dispatches as the man to take the All Blacks on tour to Europe in November. That man is Tana Umaga. Tana has done the leadership yards with Wellington and the Hurricanes. He's been the All Black vice-captain and clearly commands respect. It's logical that he should take the team away. To be honest I can't

see it being a big gamble for John Mitchell and co, either. Tana has had a couple of off-the-field hiccups but hell, he's a grown man and he knows the importance of being an All Black. He's matured greatly and wouldn't let anyone down. He's also an articulate speaker and a clued-up sort of bloke. I hope he's given the chance to show what he's made of."

He wasn't – Randell – the 1999 World Cup captain was named skipper as Mitchell and Deans rested an incredible 21 players including former skipper Thorne, Greg Feek, Dave Hewett, Greg Somerville, Corey Flynn, Mark Hammett, Tom Willis, Anton Oliver, Chris Jack, Norm Maxwell, Simon Maling, Scott Robertson, Jerry Collins, Ron Cribb, Richie McCaw, Leon MacDonald, Justin Marshall, Byron Kelleher, Caleb Ralph, Tony Brown and Aaron Mauger.

Umaga was named in the tour team and given the vice-captaincy. A few days later new Hurricanes coach Colin Cooper awarded Umaga the franchise's captaincy as well. Unlike when he was offered the provincial leadership role, Umaga didn't need time to think about the offer accepting it on the spot from Cooper. Media commitments or no media commitments, Umaga knew the value of leadership.

"It's a great honour and a privilege," he said. "I'm looking forward to it. A lot of the players have been around for a while and I feel I'm comfortable in the role. And it's a natural progression from NPC (captaincy) to Super 12."

Umaga's troubles with the new All Blacks coaches only added to his legend. The public were on his side because they'd seen him dust himself off from his personal demons and public failings to become one of the most respected men in rugby. Umaga put it all down to something as simple as maturity.

"When you turn my age, you have to (become more mature). (Leadership) has grown on me. At first I wasn't too receptive to it, but when you become an All Black, you find that people will always look up to you and you have to be a role model and show that leadership. They will give you the respect for a certain amount of time. But you don't want to lose it by doing something wrong, or mucking around. Things off the field have made me more mature as well, becoming a father for a second time. My family, my wife, getting married, that's made me grow up as well. Having that responsibility off the field has made it easier to accept that responsibility on it."

Umaga had married long-time partner Rochelle. The couple's children, son Cade and daughter Gabrielle were now nine and two respectively. He said he found home to be a refuge from rugby. "You do need to go home and chill out. I stay at home and become a dad and a husband ... that's my break away from the game." As befit his new lifestyle, Umaga again confirmed he "gave up drinking for a while" following the incident in Christchurch. "That showed me, again, that it's in your mind, if you can give it up, it's no problem. I felt good for it."

Part of this maturity was recognising some of the "political" games that were being played out through the naming of the weakened All Blacks touring party. Both he and his new skipper Randell knew the fix was on when they jetted off to England for a test at Twickenham.

"I was well and truly on the outer at the time and Tana was marginal," said Randell who'd captained the team at the 1999 World Cup. "Since Mitch had come in I'd been dropped for the end-of-year tour in 2001, started against Italy and had been a reserve against Fiji. Other than that I hadn't been on the field. Now, I was the captain... Tana and I thought it was like a set up against us to make us look bad. But we thought we're not going to go down whining and we were fired up to do well. The saying on the tour was for everyone to 'get into it'. Everyone was expecting us to get stuffed, so we said 'let's give it a good crack and have a great time along the way'. As it turned out it was great fun."

The All Blacks went close to a massive upset at Twickenham eventually losing 31-28. That was backed

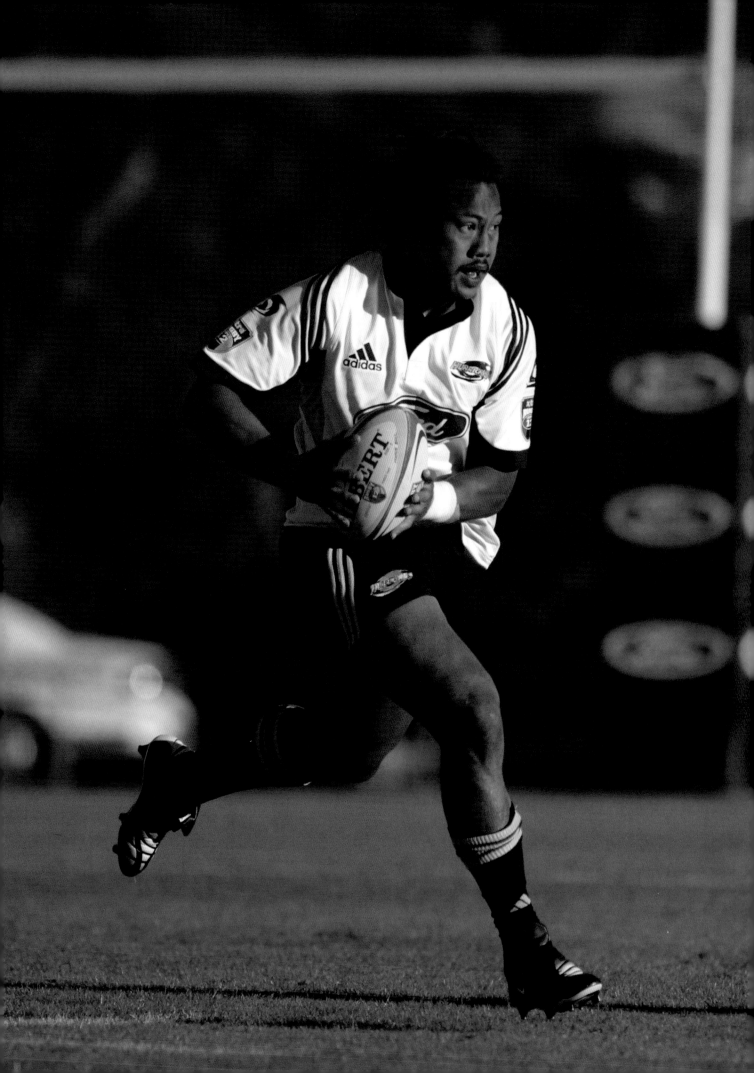

up by an unexpected 20-20 draw in Paris – where Umaga grabbed a crucial try – and an impressive 43-17 win in Cardiff. In the latter match Umaga proved his versatility by moving in one to the No 12 jersey to allow Regan King a test debut at centre.

"(Tana) has shown his best and has matured into one of the best centres in the world," Bunce said after the tour. "Who's better? Maybe Brian O'Driscoll is on a par with him, but there's no one else. I remember two seasons ago when everyone wanted him put back on the wing. Centre is a role you grow into. I see him now and he's more commanding on the field, he looks free, he's back to roaming and he's organising."

Umaga had indeed thrived on the tour. If it had been a set-up, it backfired terribly.

THE "Captain Hurricane" moniker was already taken – reserved by the team's mascot. But it was time for a rethink. There was a new captain in town. And the skipper who had been the people's choice to lead the All Blacks the previous year was at it again. Inspiring with his actions and words Tana Umaga was doing the unthinkable – leading the much maligned and oh-so-close-but-no-cigar franchise to the semi-finals for only the second time in the franchise's history.

After years of mis-management, no direction and questionable pre-season selections Hurricanes rugby was the talking point for all the right reasons in 2003. It was World Cup year and Umaga and Christian Cullen – two of the All Blacks' biggest names – were on fire.

Umaga thrived with the captaincy. It was a responsibility he took seriously. He especially enjoyed being a mentor to the young Polynesian stars in the side – players like Jerry Collins, Rodney So'oialo and Ma'a Nonu. Umaga's influence of course transcended race but there was something special about helping young Samoan players find their provincial, Super 12 and All Blacks feet.

"I enjoy being a mentor to those guys because that is what has been passed down to me before. There

have always been Polynesian players before me who have been senior players. Alama Ieremia helped me when I came in. So did Frank Bunce and Walter Little. Now I am fulfilling that role and passing things down. And not only the Polynesian boys – I am here for everyone. If these guys stick around it is up to them to pass it down. I think they realise you can learn a lot from the guys that have been involved in the All Blacks culture for a while. Zinzan Brooke, Robin Brooke, Sean Fitzpatrick… I learnt so much from them. They taught me, and now I'm passing on, what it means to be an All Black. The All Blacks' proud heritage, playing for the All Blacks and giving everything you've got – that's the message."

Nonu – who would win his first test jersey against England later in the year – soaked up all the advice and inspiration Umaga offered up.

"I admire a lot of things about Tana," said Nonu. "I admire the way he takes young fellas like me under his wing and leads us. And I respect him for the way he leads – he sets the levels for us to reach. It's easy to be inspired by him. When I was at school I looked up to him. Here was a Polynesian guy doing all the right things. Now I know there will be young Polynesian kids at school wanting to be like me. And a lot of Fijian kids wanting to be like Joe Rokocoko. That's a big responsibility. Tana doesn't let us forget that…"

Umaga had spent a lot of time on the 2002 end-of-year All Blacks tour with many of the younger players. He was determined to make the transition to All Blacks rugby easier than when he first came into an intimidating environment stacked with names like Fitzpatrick, Brooke, Bunce and Wilson.

"The difficulty when I first came into the All Blacks was that I was coming into a settled team," he said. "There were rarely any changes to the test team. There was also an experienced core of players – mostly from Auckland. When I came in they were legends. They were revered. You held them in such high esteem that often us new guys would come into that environment and say very little. But in 2003 we don't want that. We don't want guys sitting back. We can't afford to let that happen. Back when I came in you could do what you wanted. If you wanted to be the quiet guy in the corner

and say nothing, you could. You could just concentrate on your own job. And there were times when you didn't even need to do that – those guys were so good you could just get carried along. Now we need new players to feel comfortable quickly and have the confidence to express themselves."

The 'Canes had no problem expressing themselves in 2003. After a spluttering start – they lost the first two games of the season to the Crusaders and Bulls – Umaga's men went on a run of seven straight wins claiming the scalps of the Stormers, Sharks, Cats, Chiefs, Red, Waratahs and Highlanders. They lost their momentum before the semi-finals by losing their last two regular season games against the Brumbies and Blues but they were an even bet going into the playoff against the Crusaders.

Umaga was quick to heap praise on his fellow players and coach Colin Cooper. "Coops, he's straight up. He's an honest man, very refreshing, and he's instilled pride in the jersey," said Umaga. "But it's not solely him. The enthusiasm from the youth in the side keeps us older ones on our toes. There are so many young ones and they've been pushing hard. You know there's someone ready to step in. Everyone gets on well… we're a happy bunch."

The smiles disappeared after their visit to Jade Stadium and a 39-16 defeat. But the skipper had ensured he was the best midfielder in the country.

"Some of the things I went through... they are just not issues for me. They are issues for other people. If you look at them individually they aren't big issues at all and I left them behind straight after they'd happened. I moved on. I am at the stage now where I can honestly say that I don't worry about what outsiders think of me. I am not going to pretend to be someone that I'm not."

Umaga played nine games at second-five and three at centre during the Super 12. For the majority of games he played inside Nonu and the pair would be picked for the first game of international series against England.

Umaga was overlooked for the captaincy which was retained by Reuben Thorne. And publicly at least he wasn't showing any disappointment. "A lot of patience is required to be All Black captain because it is a very pressurised job," Umaga said. "I like to stick to myself without the gaze of everyone. I have been a fan of (Thorne's) ever since he came into the All Blacks. He leads us the way he does. He doesn't say much but you don't have to as long as you're doing your job. He's the right man to do the job. He doesn't ask for anything; he just goes out and does it himself. I'm more animated than he is. Sometimes I don't chew over my words and don't know what I'm spitting out but that's the way I am. He's a deeper thinker than I am."

Unfortunately for the Umaga/Nonu partnership there was very little action against England. When the backline did get the ball they squandered any chance of rhythm with dropped balls and forward passes. And up front it was uglier with the All Blacks forward pack unable to take advantage of a six-man England pack when they had two players in the sin-bin. England won the game 15-13 and with a tick under four months until the beginning of the World Cup nervousness invaded the rugby nation.

A week later the All Blacks were back in business against Wales. An injury to the Crusaders' No 12 Aaron Mauger allowed Dan Carter to come into the test team pushing Umaga back into Nonu's centre jersey.

The new midfield pairing would spend the next 160 minutes together as the All Blacks dispatched Wales (55-3) and France (31-23). The pairing was a good one but once Mauger was back to full fitness – in time for the Tri-nations – the sublime rugby the team had promised for so long finally arrived. The backline of Justin Marshall, Carlos Spencer, Joe Rokocoko,

Mauger, Umaga, Doug Howlett and Mils Muliaina the best in the business.

The team went to Pretoria and won 52-16 and seven days later walloped the Wallabies 50-21. The backs had combined for 13 tries against two of the world's powerhouses. Umaga was a key to the effectiveness of the play – offering the perfect link to the wings, a loose-forward mentality when required to bust over the advantage line and brutal defence.

And it was that "D" that had him being talked about as the world's best centre after he helped inspire 19-11 and 21-17 wins against the 'Boks and Wallabies on New Zealand soil as the Tri-nations and Bledisloe Cups were won.

The test in Sydney was a significant one for Umaga – it was his 50th. Typically he underplayed it – "Every game for the All Blacks is a privilege. The one I look forward to most is the next one. I'm looking forward to my 51st."

It was left to his teammates to pay the tributes. Halfback Justin Marshall had played with Umaga since the Wellingtonian made his All Blacks' debut in 1997. He said Umaga is "a very humble person and a proud All Black. And proud All Blacks always put the team first and give their utmost for the side. Personal milestones get put aside. Tana hasn't mentioned it once this week. But, having said that, it is still an amazing effort and something he will be proud of once he's stopped playing. He's a senior member of the team (and offers leadership). But if I was selecting a side, I'd pick him on pure talent. He's quick, he's got all the qualities, and as a centre, he's one of the best we've ever had. Anyone can bring a bit of experience, what Tana brings is his talent, whether it's his 50th test or his 15th."

Before the World Cup began Umaga was linked to a move to Japanese club Toyota at the end of 2003. Both Umaga and his agent Rob Brady denied the story but a contract with Umaga's name on it was sent to Brady by Toyota's Errol Brain – the former Counties and

NZ Maori captain. It was an unnecessary distraction but a further sign of Umaga's growing worldwide reputation. He was the "superstar" in the All Blacks. And how he went would determine how the All Blacks went in Australia as they chased their first World Cup triumph since 1987.

And Umaga was in an upbeat mood before the tournament, convinced that the lessons of 1999 had been learnt. He certainly hadn't forgotten the country's reaction to the semi-final loss against the French. He told the *Sunday Star Times'* Chris Mirams: "I did notice people's reaction. They would talk to each other behind their hand and things. There was an uneasy feeling for a while but I tried to put it behind me. There were lessons learned which I have never forgotten. Sometimes you just can't control everything whether it's a rugby game or life. If we give our all and do our best we might not get the result but I don't think there's any reason to feel bad if we've given all we've got. If you've done that, you've just been beaten by a better team."

The All Blacks chances were immediately on tenterhooks following the opening game of the tournament against Italy. Mitchell had decided to invest in youth and had left behind experienced pros Christian Cullen, Andrew Mehrtens and Anton Oliver. And within 23 minutes of the opener – which would be won 70-7 – they now looked to be without Umaga too after he collided with Spencer and tore ligaments in his left knee.

The next five weeks were dominated by a "will he or won't he" debate about Umaga's ability to play again in the tournament. The debate hit fever pitch before the quarter-final against the Springboks in Sydney after Canada (68-6), Tonga (91-7) and Wales (53-37) had been dispatched.

Nonu was given the start against the Canadians but it was clear that World Cup rugby was beyond him and the No 13 jersey was handed to Leon MacDonald who couldn't displace Muliania at fullback. MacDonald

was solid on attack but lacked the individual skill to spark an attack and the mongrel to nullify one on defence. The All Blacks needed Umaga but he failed a fitness test three days out of the South African game.

MacDonald put in his best performance at the World Cup scoring a try and kicking three penalties as the All Blacks won through to a semi-final date with Australia with a 29-9 victory. And the Canterbury fullback-cum-centre was quick to praise Umaga for his off-field assistance.

"Tana has taken a bit of interest in the way I've been playing," MacDonald said. "He has offered me a few tips. I have been really thankful for that. There were things I was working on last week that he has given me advice on. That is the nature of the team – everyone is concentrating on things that can help the team and there is no selfishness. We are all here to help each other. Tana is a great player at making the tackle, getting to his feet and stealing the ball. So I've been working on things like that."

Five days out of the game against Australia it was reported that All Blacks doctor John Mayhew had suggested Umaga would be fit and available for selection for the game on November 15. But two days later Mitchell named the side and Umaga's name was missing. "It's been pretty close to five to six weeks since he's played any rugby," Mitchell told a packed press conference. "He's just not sharp enough, I couldn't put it any clearer than that. You have to be sharp at this level. That comes through speed and quickness and alertness."

Ironically the All Blacks would have none of those qualities in the semi-final, losing 22-10. After the defeat – and the meaningless win in the third and fourth place play off – Umaga would not be drawn on whether he felt fit to play in the semifinal. "It's irrelevant. I don't want to say anything. I didn't play, we didn't get the result, everyone's gutted and we just have to live with it."

Asked this year whether he could have played or not Umaga was still playing it straight. "I felt I was at my best in 2003 but I only lasted 21 minutes. Could I have played the semi-final? Any player will tell you that, if asked, they'll play. It comes down to the coaches. I don't think I was 100 per cent but I would have walked on there with crutches if I could have. It's what you live for. You train so hard and long for it. They went for a player that was 100 per cent."

A week after the semi-final Umaga , who was "not sharp enough" for a game of rugby was playing for the Wainuiomata club's 4C one-day cricket side against Upper Hutt at Trentham. Showing no signs of his knee injury, his medium pacers garnered three wickets for 11 from his four overs... *Howzat!*

THE LEGACY

FROM coaches and teammates you have heard the testimonials about his character and his commitment and with your eyes you've seen his steady, unselfish and sometimes spectacular play. But some still doubted Tana Umaga.

They'd gaze with some uncertainty at his dreadlocks, his goatee and his scowl; they remember him as the young inconsistent tearaway who debuted for Wellington in 1994. And in their mind's eye they see him on their television screen stumbling through a Christchurch street in 2000. They wonder: When will Mr Hyde show up again and ruin all Dr Jekyll's recent good work?

WHEN the phone rang in mid-March Tana Umaga was still in bed. The last thing he wanted in the midst of another struggling Hurricanes season was to miss out on something he could control – sleep. When his wife Rochelle told him it was new All Blacks coach Graham Henry on the other end of the phone he didn't believe her. A few minutes later Umaga hung up the phone and relayed the news to the mother of his two children… Henry had just asked him to be the 59th captain of the All Blacks.

"I've had to ask him since to reconfirm it's me he wants," Umaga said as he sat alongside Henry when he was unveiled as the new skipper. Only Rochelle, his manager Rob Brady and older brother Mike had known the announcement was imminent. He let the rest of his family in on the secret at a dinner at his sister's home in Wainuiomata a day earlier.

Umaga had been an All Black since 1997, playing under skippers Sean Fitzpatrick, Taine Randell, Anton Oliver, Todd Blackadder and Reuben Thorne. Having seen what they endured in the harsh spotlight that goes with the job, he did not say yes to Henry without considering the impact on Rochelle and children Cade, (then 10) and Gabrielle (then 4).

"I didn't say yes straight away when Graham asked me to be captain. I had to talk it over with my wife, Rochelle. She plays a big part in my life. As captain you are under the spotlight. And the demands are more than if you are in the team as a player."

The move saw Umaga become just the second back to lead the All Blacks since halfback David Kirk won the World Cup in 1987. Another halfback Justin Marshall briefly held the mantle in 1997 as Sean Fitzpatrick struggled with a knee injury. Wing Stu Wilson was the last player to lead the All Blacks from the outside backs, in 1983.

The man Umaga deposed as skipper moved quickly to support the new captain. And Reuben Thorne – who had joined Gary Whetton, Sean Fitzpatrick and Taine Randell as All Blacks leaders who

had failed to win the World Cup – offered some sage advice to the players' new boss. He admitted some aspects of the job he found "burdensome". Throughout his tenure he was unfairly maligned in some media sectors for not being a more high-profile leader. He insisted that it "never really got to me".

Thorne said captains were always constantly learning. "Particularly with the All Blacks, it's helluva difficult. You're put in a situation where you have a lot of challenges and you just have to learn to deal with it. It puts some extra pressure on you. There are a lot of other things you have to deal with outside pure rugby circles. It can be burdensome, particularly if things aren't going well. (But) it only bothers you as much as you let it bother you…"

Henry's move to empower Umaga was met with widespread approval.

Wilson – who captained the team in three tests – was a long time supporter of Umaga's and was thrilled. "During a career that's reached dizzy heights (and a few lows) Tana Umaga has always shown me he's been incredibly proud to pull on the black jersey. Like all of us he believes it's a privilege, not a right, to be an All Black and that's come through during his career. I like the fact that he's the best player in his position because with all due respect to the previous captain, that wasn't the situation."

More importantly though Henry was adamant he'd chosen the right man. Wayne Smith – who made Umaga his "unofficial" vice-captain in 2001 – was back with the All Blacks as an assistant coach alongside former Canterbury and Wales coach Steve Hansen. And despite Smith having links to Canterbury and the Crusaders, neither second-guessed Henry when it came to replacing Thorne with Umaga.

"Tana is a very positive role model for New Zealand rugby," Henry said. "He is highly respected by his teammates, knows the game well and is a world-class player. He has a huge amount of experience. We talked about it as a group of selectors. There was

"Every time I really sat down and actually had a long think about it I realised I had to do what was best for my family more than myself, with two young children.
(But) I always felt the best place to bring the kids up was here, so that's pretty much why I think I stayed here in the end."

a unanimous decision that this was the way to move forward. There was a lot of spadework done before the decision was made."

For his part Umaga vowed not to change his leadership style. He said he was a captain who led from the front, letting his actions speak louder than words. He also relied heavily on senior players in the team. It was a style that had worked for him as captain of the Hurricanes.

"I won't change my style. They have picked me for who I am and to go away from that will be to go away from who they have picked. Hopefully, we will have a bit more luck than I've had with the Hurricanes. Captaincy is something that has really come upon me. When I was younger I never wanted to be captain of anything. I just wanted to play. It is something I have grown into. I've felt I've grown up a lot in the last few years. It is a maturing thing. You get enough experience to handle the rigors of it.

"Wayne Smith remembers making me vice-captain. He remembers what I said to him that day, that I didn't like being vice-captain because it hurts too much the next day when you lose. That is why it's tough. The next day you hurt even more – it lingers. But I'm happy with that responsibility now. It makes me stronger and makes me want to not have that feeling again. It's also helped me know the game a lot better."

Umaga said he would try to employ the best qualities of the captains he has played under. "Leading from the front and living what you say are important," he said. "You can't say something and then go and do the opposite. It's important to have good relationships with everyone. It doesn't matter how long you have been in the team. Those are the main things. I try to keep it simple. I don't try to get outside of my area. If I can't do it, I can't do it. I just have to keep it real."

Fundamentally one of the key attributes Umaga had that Henry admired was his willingness to share the leadership role. Some captains want total control.

Umaga didn't. "(It's about) more actions than words for me," Umaga said. "That is why I need the other senior players to come on board so they can take up some of the workload in the speaking stakes. If I'm doing all the talking and all the yelling, it is a bit like a teacher. If players hear you yelling all the time then often they'll turn off. We need as many voices as we can – sending the same message. It's more powerful than coming from the same person."

That fit perfectly with Henry's plans to introduce leadership groups. Other coaches had talked about "growing leaders" but Henry was the first to do something about it. Along with his management group – headed by new All Blacks manager Darren Shand – a large group of players were put into the leadership group. At times the numbers in the group would swell to 12 and during Henry's reign have included players like Jerry Collins, Jono Gibbes, Carl Hayman, Doug Howlett, Chris Jack, Byron Kelleher, Richie McCaw, Leon MacDonald, Justin Marshall, Aaron Mauger, Keven Mealamu, Andrew Mehrtens, Mils Muliaina, Anton Oliver, Xavier Rush, Greg Somerville, Rodney So'oialo and Moses Tuiali'i.

Umaga's Samoan roots were all-important as well. While not a reason to be given the captaincy the reality is the All Blacks are dominated by brown players. The majority are Polynesian and for them Umaga's story was one they could relate to. Like most of them, Umaga had used rugby as his passport out of a less than perfect childhood.

"I knew from a young age that sport was my talent and I did everything I could to make sure it was

my way out," said Umaga who was raised in Homedale – a place known as The Village at the southern end of Wainuiomata near the entrance to Moore's Valley. Now he lives over the hill in Woburn – Lower Hutt's most expensive suburb – but he's grateful for the breaks Wainuiomata gave him and for the friends he still has there.

"My mum and dad made me and they worked really hard for us," he told the *Dominion*, "but Wainui's environment also helped make me. The people that I associated with grew up hard and it rubs off on you."

During his time in Wainui, Umaga mixed with "people who were doing life tough" but they always did the best they could for their families. "That's what's stuck with me," said Umaga who would play sport on Saturdays and join his parents Falefasa and Tauese at the Congregation Church of American Samoa in Parkway on Sundays. "They did the best with what they had and that's what it's about here. We are a low socio-economic area here. I feel we are a very tight community and there are a lot of tough times, none more so than now..."

There would be tough times ahead for the All Blacks in 2004 as well but this was a time of huge significance. "He personally embodies the contemporary ethos of the New Zealand game," wrote Chris Laidlaw. "Umaga is a genuine superstar, someone who has earned that status by an unbeatable combination of talent, willpower and the quality of his personality. But it goes further than that. Umaga is an example of the power of sport to bring out the latent qualities in an individual who might otherwise have ended up at the wrong end of the social stick. A Polynesian Kiwi from the modesty of Petone, he has grown so profoundly as a player and as a personality that he now dominates the All Black landscape so much that it is almost unthinkable for him not to be there.

"He started, like so many young Polynesian players, without a clue as to what it takes to be a successful international sportsman. He learned the hard way. In and out of the Wellington team in the early 90s after a flirtation with league, he looked like your typical on again/off again winger. But then Alama Ieremia got hold of him. Ieremia was not your average local boy. He was Samoan-born and the natural leader among Wellington's Samoan players. He helped Umaga to realise that with more application and more self-discipline he could do just about anything he liked in rugby.

"And he has done just that. When they gave him his chance on the wing for the All Blacks he grabbed it and, with Jonah Lomu, constituted as potent a pairing on the wings as has probably ever walked a rugby field. Umaga was forced to walk in Jonah's shadow for several years but, gradually, the world and the All Black selectors began to realise that he was considerably more irreplaceable in the All Blacks than Jonah and he has since proved that point beyond question."

Now, as the first Polynesian captain of the All Blacks… the power of that particular imagery in this country was, and is, untold. Players, coaches, administrators, sponsors and media gravitated towards him. Tana Umaga had become something akin to the pied piper. The question was, would he lead us to glory or more, unbearable, pain.

All Blacks supporters didn't have to wait long to find out. First up in the Umaga/Henry era was the World Cup champions England – although the England that Sir Clive Woodward brought Down Under in 2004

beared little resemblance to the team that beat Australia to lift the William Webb Ellis trophy. World Cup stars Jonny Wilkinson and Martin Johnson led a list of 14 absentees. But Woodward, who would return a year later with the British Lions, was talking a good talk before the first of the two tests in Dunedin.

"We're not hiding. It will be England's strongest team next Saturday," Woodward said. "Test match rugby is about the next test. For the last World Cup, we never planned for the World Cup. We went match by match. I don't think we had any game in those four years where we didn't pick our strongest team. We came here full strength (last year) and we won the test match. That's what we're going to try to do next weekend."

Umaga spent the night before the test with his wife and children. He received dozens of "good luck" messages including a fax from Prime Minister Helen Clark. But publicly he wasn't reflective. There were no interviews about where he'd come from or what he'd overcome to be here – captaining the All Blacks. For Umaga it was more of a *Let's get it on* mentality.

And they did – the All Blacks cruising to a comprehensive 36-3 win. Umaga taunted Woodward immediately after the game when he said the All Blacks "will be better". And, while the scoreline didn't show it, they did. The second test was won 36-12 and the rugby nation was buoyed by how Umaga's troops responded to the cheap shots coming in from England's players. When Simon Shaw stomped on All Black lock Keith Robinson the offending player was immediately set upon by New Zealanders keen to support their mate. And Umaga, when Shaw was shown the red card, let out a scream of delight as he stood by Shaw and the referee delivering the news.

Umaga celebrated the win by signing a new deal with the NZRU which tied him to New Zealand rugby through to the end of the 2007 World Cup. "Every time I really sat down and actually had a long think about it I realised I had to do what was best for my

family more than myself, with two young children," said Umaga who confirmed he entertained the idea of playing overseas. "(But) I always felt the best place to bring the kids up was here, so that's pretty much why I think I stayed here in the end." When talking to the *Dominion* a candid Umaga revealed he had narrowed a swag of lucrative overseas offers that had been "good for the ego" down to two, in France and Japan – all but confirming the offer from Toyota that was denied before the 2003 World Cup. "I can't name the clubs, but one was to go to France and the other to Japan. From my perspective I wanted to go to France. More so because it was tougher rugby and the opportunity to play in the Heineken Cup. There has been a lot of talk about which is tougher, Heineken Cup or Super 12 and I wanted to try it out and make my own decision."

The next outings for the team before the battle for the Tri-nations and Bledisloe Cups were tests against Argentina and the Pacific Islands in Hamilton and Albany respectively. Both tests were won – 41-7 against the Pumas and 41-26 against the Islanders – but neither win was convincing. But Umaga – who scored a try in both games – had galvanised the country's supporters. Not since the days of Sean Fitzpatrick had a captain been so popular nationwide. Taine Randell – who replaced Fitzpatrick in 1998 never enjoyed total support because of his quiet on-field demeanor. Todd Blackadder was loved in the South Island and despised by many in the North Island. Reuben Thorne was loved in Canterbury and nowhere else. Umaga though transcended all. The public was used to him. They'd seen him in action since 1994. They felt like they knew him. Knew that they could trust him.

Umaga's stakes certainly raised midway through 2004 with the release of the All Blacks' World Cup doctor John Mayhew's book *Rugby's Medicine Man* and his take on Umaga's injury. He said that Umaga was fit enough to be considered for selection before the end of the pool matches.

"That was where I believe the mistake was made," he wrote. "Had we taken the risk on Tana in the final pool game against Wales, perhaps by including him on the bench and giving him a run towards the end, we'd have known exactly where we were with him. His knee wouldn't have been any worse for the 'experiment', and if it hadn't worked out, we could have called for a replacement. However, if he'd got through OK, we'd have increased our midfield options for the knockout section of the tournament while reintroducing a huge amount of leadership and experience to the fold.

"By not trialing Tana against Wales, we virtually ruled him out of further participation in the tournament, and his on-field presence was sorely missed at Telstra Stadium. The coaches' rationale for leaving Tana out of the equation was that he lacked sharpness and wasn't ready. To be fair to them, they were working on the advice of the team's training staff, but it did seem to me that a double standard was being applied. We had, after all, nursed Aaron Mauger along when he was struggling with injury and far from full match fitness. Corey Flynn had also been selected in the squad ahead of Anton Oliver when he hadn't had a lot of rugby behind him because of injury."

And Umaga – seen as hard done-by the masses – only helped his relationship with his public through honesty once he had the captaincy. After the win against Argentina he berated himself publicly after questioning Australian official Stuart Dickinson during the test. He admitted he was becoming too vocal towards referees and said he had given thought to changing his approach. "I'm trying to be more calm in confronting the ref. It's normal when you come up against someone who's ranting and raving in your face just to switch off. I'm trying my best and we'll see how we go."

Umaga's public had plenty to be happy about after the opening Tri-nations game. A 16-7 win against the Wallabies in Wellington ensured the All Blacks held onto the Bledisloe Cup for another year. And while,

again, the performance was at best average, there was enough being shown by the side to retain the faith of the majority.

The game's hardest ever player All Black great Colin Meads had backed Umaga after the test after – just as in the England game – players stood up for each other when Justin Marshall and Carlos Spencer took to Australian hooker Brendan Cannon after he punched Keven Mealamu. "I've been waiting to see a performance like that for a long time," Meads told *Sunday News*. "If any of your mates are getting knocked around you have to stand up for them. That's why you are called a team and this lot are proving they are a team and they are not going to back down to anyone. It would be hard not to like this All Blacks team."

The All Blacks were back in action seven days later in Christchurch against the Springboks. They needed a last minute try from wing Doug Howlett to escape with a 23-21 win.

Two wins from two games, the Bledisloe Cup locked away from another summer… it was the perfect start for Umaga's stint in-charge. Things though went bad quickly for the All Blacks.

As the All Blacks arrived in Sydney to the test at Homebush Stadium they knew a win would secure the Tri-nations title. Umaga – while not distracted from his duties – was on edge because Rochelle was expecting their third child at any time. Aaron Mauger, who was battling back from a knee injury, was put on stand-by.

As it was Mauger was not needed – although he could have been used. Dan Carter – a first-five – was in at second-five, the only change from the backline that ran in seven tries against the Wallabies a year earlier. This time though the backs fired blanks and stumbled to a 23-18 loss.

If Umaga wasn't distracted before the game, he certainly was after it. He was on the first plane to Wellington to witness Rochelle give birth to Lily-Kate Umaga at Hutt Hospital. The next morning, at 6.30am,

"Parents as first teachers is something I firmly believe in…
I have an 11-year-old son who has just started a new school.
I come home from training a bit tired. I am forcing myself
to get up and help him with his homework.
I have my first meeting with my son's teacher next week.
I will try to attend that, which will be the first one in a while."

he was on his way to join the team in Johannesburg. And in addition to the newest member of his family to occupy his mind on the long-haul flight was the knowledge that the All Blacks were at the centre of a bizarre Osama bin Laden terrorist threat.

South African reports suggested bombers from al Qaeda planned to blow up Ellis Park – the South African ground where they were due to play the Springboks. The bombing plot was eventually rumbled when two South African terror suspects were busted with one of bin Laden's top men in Pakistan. During interrogation, the trio confessed to planning a series of bomb attacks, including the one at Ellis Park.

While there were no terrorists involved, the All Blacks were "attacked" in Johannesburg as they crashed to a 40-26 loss. South Africa's 23-19 triumph against Australia in Durban a week later would see them confirmed as Tri-nations champions. The All Blacks had to settle for last place.

Umaga emerged from the campaign relatively unscathed. Only Zinzan Brooke – the great All Black backrower of the 90s now based in England – signaled Umaga out for an all out attack. "Ever since (Umaga) has taken the captaincy, I don't think Tana has been as confident in his play," said Brooke, who won 58 test caps with the All Blacks between 1987 and 1997. "He's more worried about the other stuff that goes with being a captain rather than concentrating on his game. I actually think he has been a bit flat. I think they should take the captaincy off him and get him back to playing the way he was before he took up the job. The captaincy role is a lot to take on. I know he is an experienced player, but just because you have been there for 10 years doesn't necessarily mean that you are going to be a good captain."

Brooke though was very much a lone wolf. Any pressure that came on from within New Zealand was focused on the coaching staff and subsequently a number of international playing careers would come to a forced end. Carlos Spencer, Xavier Rush

and Andrew Mehrtens wouldn't be sighted in black again.

And it wasn't only the media putting the heat on. Less than a month after the Ellis Park failure Umaga used a luncheon in Brisbane to have a crack at the All Blacks' impotent flat backline. And while he didn't mean to attack Mehrtens or Spencer he said the flat backline would be an instant success with Wallabies playmaker Stephen Larkham running the show. The controversial flat backline attack had been widely criticised after the All Blacks scored only five tries in four matches, compared to 17 in the tournament the previous year when John Mitchell had control of the team.

"If you really wanted to have that kind of backline you need a five-eighth like Stephen Larkham, who, I feel, is the best running five-eighth in the world at the moment," said Umaga who believed Spencer and Mehrtens were not given enough time by Henry to adapt. "They're great players, but to be playing one style for all your life and then in the space of three or four weeks to be told to play another way, you just can't do it. It's going to take time for those guys to develop that. At the moment, if you could put one player in there who could spark it straight away it's (Larkham) with the style that he plays."

In this world of politically correct nonsense it would have been expected that Umaga would have been widely criticised for making such statements. Whether he intended to or not, he was giving the All Blacks' No 10s a public serve. But it didn't seem to matter when it came to Umaga because the rugby public largely agreed with him. And it was agreed by scribes at the time that Umaga should be able to criticise because he was never averse to pointing the finger at himself. "I just needed to get away from the game a little bit," said Umaga when quizzed about how he dealt with the team's failure. "It's as mental as it is physical really. Having the captaincy with the All Blacks was great, but I took the losses hard. I took them personally and it took me a while to put them behind me. I had to mourn those losses because it really did affect me and obviously my performance in that last game was not up to my standards."

Umaga would have a chance at redemption on the end-of-year tour to Italy, Wales and France. Before the tour though *Sunday News* revealed that Richie McCaw – the Canterbury and Crusaders No 7 – would captain the team against the Welsh. The story fanned flames that suggested that Brooke's suggestion was being seriously considered by Henry and his fellow selectors. But it wasn't. When Umaga took on the captaincy he agreed to do the job for two years. Both Henry and Umaga knew his body wouldn't last through to 2007 and part of Umaga's role would be to groom McCaw. The test against the under-strength Welsh was the perfect opportunity to pass the captain's torch – albeit temporarily – to McCaw.

But before that would happen the All Blacks had a test against Italy in Rome. Umaga's mentoring ability came to the fore when, from second-five, he nursed his Wellington teammate Conrad Smith through his first test. Inside him in the No 10 jersey was another star in the making, Dan Carter. He had been involved in the All Blacks since 2003 but with Spencer and Mehrtens banished, the All Blacks backline was his to run. And run it he did as the New Zealanders romped to a 59-10 victory – Umaga and McCaw each scoring two tries.

Aaron Mauger slipped into Umaga's No 12 jersey in Cardiff with his Crusaders teammate Casey Laulala outside him. And while the combination was solid there was little doubt that the midfield missed Umaga's defence and general leadership. And when McCaw's team scrapped through with only a 26-25 win there was no doubt that Umaga would return against the French in Paris.

And what a return it would be. Umaga – with an intimate knowledge of the two-year deal he's struck with Henry – had been frustrated with how McCaw's

elevation in Cardiff had been interpreted as the beginning of his end. He was determined to end the year on both a personal and team high. He decided to lead literally from start to end as he took on the responsibility of leading the haka for the first time in his career. "I've had feedback from my wife (Rochelle, who is Maori) and she said it was good, so that's always positive," he said. "We were told that the words do mean a bit but it's how you go about it, and the feeling and passion that comes from within (that matters). Hopefully I gave it everything I had."

There is no doubt that this was one of the most motivated All Blacks teams of recent years. The All Blacks wore a red poppy on their right shoulder at Stade de France to honour Armistice and the memory of New Zealand soldiers who had died in battle in Europe. Chief among their thoughts was Dave Gallaher, the wing forward who captained Originals when they toured Europe in 1906 and later fought in World War I and died from his wounds at Passchendaele. Born in Ireland, Gallagher was nearly 44 when he died on October 4, 1917, and the All Blacks visited his grave at a war cemetery in Belgium in 2000. Since the test against France in Paris that year they have played for the Dave Gallaher Trophy. They won that inaugural match and have kept the trophy ever since. "We can't take his body back but we take his memory back in the trophy we play for," Umaga said before the game.

And there was never any doubt the trophy would head home again as tries to Rodney So'oialo, Jerry Collins, Byron Kelleher and Ma'a Nonu along with Carter's 25 points (four conversions, four penalties and a try) delivered a record 46-6 win. The All Blacks' performance had a big impact on the French media. Headlines in national sports daily paper *L'Equipe* such as La Maree Noire (The Black Tide) and La Punition Black (The Black Punishment) conveyed the general feeling towards one of the worst ever defeats of the French.

With the French out of the way and only a meaningless game against the Barbarians at Twickenham left to play before the All Blacks headed home, the focus immediately turned to 2005 and the Lions tour. The build up to the tour – the most hyped in New Zealand history – would have a massive impact on Umaga's legacy. Because, coupled with his performance in Paris, while the team was filming a television commercial for adidas in England it dawned on Umaga and other senior All Blacks that they were being over commericalised. They understood that without adidas they wouldn't be on their telephone number pay packets and without the likes of News Limited there wouldn't be any meaningful competitions to play in year-in-year-out. But the one thing they controlled – other than performance – was the haka.

Sick of having to perform *Ka Mate!* for endless print and television advertisements the team's leadership group – led by Umaga – began taking back control of when and where the haka would be performed. They would eventually inform All Blacks manager Darren Shand that they wouldn't perform *Ka Mate!* for any more advertising campaigns – the team believing the haka was for them, no one else. That led to discussions within the team about moving away from *Ka Mate!* and composing a new haka that incorporated the changing face of the team. *Ka Mate!* tells the story of Te Rauparaha – it has no literal meaning for the team's Samoan, Tongan, Fijian and European players.

It was out of that frustration that *Kapa o Pango* was born. The controversial haka – and it throat slitting action – was composed by Ngati Porou's Derek Lardelli. While *Ka Mate!* certainly has its place in All Blacks history, the modern-day All Black was aware the translation had little meaning to them as All Blacks.

Slap the hands against the thighs. Puff out the chest. Bend the knees. Let the hip follow. Stamp the feet as hard as you can. It is death! It is death! It is life! It is life! This is the hairy person who *caused the sun to shine. Keep abreast! Keep abreast. The rank! Hold fast! Into the sun that shines!*

Lardelli's *Kapa o Pango* resonated with the players because it was about them. For them.

Kapa o Pango kia whakawhenua au i ahau! (Let me become one with the land.) **Hi aue, hi! Ko Aotearoa e ngunguru nei!** (This is our land that rumbles.) **Au, au, aue ha!** (And it's my time! It's my moment!) **Ko Kapa o Pango e ngunguru nei!** (This defines us as the All Blacks) **Au, au, aue ha!** (It's my time! It's my moment! **I ahaha! Ka tu te ihiihi** (Our dominance.) **Ka tu te wanawana** (Our supremacy will triumph.) **Ki runga ki te rangi e tu iho nei, tu iho nei, hi!** (And will be placed on high.) **Ponga ra!** (Silver fern!) **Kapa o Pango, aue hi!** (All Blacks!) **Ponga ra!** (Silver fern!) **Kapa o Pango, aue hi, ha!** (All Blacks!)

It was debuted against the South Africans in the 2005 Tri-nations but a year later Umaga revealed he had wanted it performed for the first time against the Lions. "We actually wanted to use the new haka during the Lions series but we had a bit of reluctance from the younger guys, which was rightly so too, because they hadn't even played a test yet and they were asking to be involved in changing the haka," Umaga said.

There is little doubt Umaga was a driving force behind the change. As the team's captain he would often be asked to perform the haka every time he showed up at an official function. And he was frustrated with the over-use of *Ka Mate!* by other sporting groups and the lack of understanding and respect shown to it. At least with *Kapa o Pango* there could be no argument about which group of men should be able to perform it – the All Blacks and the All Blacks alone.

After the haka had its first airing there was widespread condemnation of the throat-cutting motion at the end of *Kapa o Pango*. It was, predictably, interpreted as the All Blacks saying something akin to **We are going to kill you!** to their opponents.

The official line of course came from Lardelli who said that *Kapa o Pango* ends with the word 'Ha' which translates as the breath of life. The words and motions represent drawing vital energy into the heart and lungs. The right arm searches for the 'Ha' on the left side of the body, Lardelli explained, while the head turns to the right also symbolically seeking vital energy. The right hand hauls that energy into the pou-whakaora (the heart, lungs and air passages), then the eyes and tongue signal that the energy has been harnessed before it is expelled with the final 'Ha'.

While *Kapa o Pango* wouldn't be performed for the Lions, its violent nature would be replicated in the first minute of the first test of one of history's most controversial rugby moments.

FITTINGLY it was the Scottish dramatist and novelist James Barrie who first said *Life is a long lesson in humility*. It was one of those life lessons that Sir Clive Woodward – the coach of the British and Irish Lions – would learn on his disastrous foray onto these shores in 2005. And while Barrie – who wrote and directed *Peter Pan* in 1904 – wasn't around the see the clash of rugby giants, if he had been, he may have been inspired to pen one or two more quotable quotes. *Mess with our skipper at your peril!* would have been the perfect way to sum up Woodward's mischievous attempts to destabilise Tana Umaga.

Umaga had started 2005 the way he'd finished 2004 – fending off talk of retirement. As he prepared for the Super 12 he attempted to quell the rumors when he told the *Dominion* he would leave on his terms. "You get old, that's just the way it is and you can't beat Father Time. In my early days I wasn't the fittest player and wasn't in the condition I am now. I'm probably in the best condition, physically and mentally, to withstand professional rugby. I still enjoy playing, and playing at this level. I'm a competitor. I don't know if I could go back and play club rugby. I don't know if I'd last – or if people would last long playing with me."

Though Umaga noted "everyone's waiting for me to go" he was confident he would know when the time has come to retire and that he would get out on his own terms. "That's the kind of person I am – I like having the last word. It's about knowing when that is. It will hit me – or someone will tell me – but I'd like to think I can go on my own terms."

His terms meant "as a winner". And with the Lions tour, the Bledisloe Cup, Tri-nations and a shot at a Grand Slam tour at the end of the year the stage was set for the perfect farewell.

Before the All Blacks season began however Umaga had some business to take care of in the Super 12. The team would go on to lose to the Crusaders in a semi-final at Jade Stadium. Making it to the playoffs would have been the highlight of any other Hurricanes campaign but not this time. That came at Eden Park when the Hurricanes beat the Blues in Auckland for the first time. And motivating the team that night was a *Do it for Tana* call from his teammates as their skipper brought up his 100th Super 12 appearance. "That was for T," Jerry Collins said after the game. It was a show of loyalty and respect from the 'Canes – something that would soon be replicated by his All Blacks charges.

Before the main event of the domestic season – the Lions tour – there was the formality of a test against Fiji to get out of the way. A 91-0 win did very little for the All Blacks build up to the first test against Woodward's Lions in Christchurch other than offer up a debut to the devastatingly good wing Sitiveni Sivivatu and young Otago lock James Ryan.

While the hype before the first Lions test was at fever-pitch, that's all it was. *Hype*. It was clear even before the Lions arrived in New Zealand they didn't have the personnel to beat the All Blacks. Laurie Mains, writing in his column in the *Sunday News*, called them the worst Lions team in 55 years. "The 1966 and 1983 Lions were beaten 4-0 by the All Blacks and Woodward's team doesn't appear to have better players than those teams," Mains wrote. "If the Lions perform

at the level they showed in the draw against Argentina (played the week before they arrived in New Zealand) they are likely to be beaten in New Zealand in several provincial games as well as be hammered in the tests."

Not even the inclusion of England's World Cup hero Jonny Wilkinson had Mains worried. "Wilkinson is a very fine player. Under normal circumstances he would have been a significant factor. But the Lions are not going to be close enough to the All Blacks for Wilko to have a great deal of effect."

Another All Blacks legend, 117-game veteran Andy Haden, had blasted Woodward's decision to bring a record 45 players on tour. He said it was a nightmare scenario. "Realistically, disappointment is only just around the corner for close to half of this team. There will be at least 20 who won't make it on to the field in a test match. Some scribe will find a player with complaints, because some won't get enough game time to have made it worthwhile leaving London."

And former All Blacks coach John Mitchell – who had an intimate knowledge of many of the players in the Lions squad from his days as Woodward's England assistant – joined Mains, Haden, Sean Fitzpatrick and Zinzan Brooke in predicting a 3-0 blackwash.

And the Lions did nothing to offer their supporters any hope once they started playing in New Zealand. After failing to inspire in their wins against Bay of Plenty and Taranaki, the Lions lost to the NZ Maori in Hamilton 19-13. Wins against Wellington, Otago and Southland followed but at no time did Woodward – desperate to keep some aces up his sleeve – have his best XV on the field.

In contrast, the All Blacks side was a settled one. Sivivatu had replaced the out of touch Joe Rokocoko on the wing and Leon MacDonald had returned from a stint in Japan to hold off Mils Muliaina's challenge for the fullbacks berth. Otherwise it was a team full of experience playing together. And that would tell in the end as the All Blacks went 1-0 up in the three tests series with a 21-3 win.

But any celebrations were put on ice after Umaga and hooker Keven Mealamu were involved in an incident with the Lions skipper Brian O'Driscoll in the first minute of the encounter. The All Blacks would say they were "cleaning out" at a ruck. The Lions would say O'Driscoll was the victim of a spear tackle. Regardless of intent or no intent the result was that O'Driscoll was out of the test and out of the tour with a dislocated shoulder injury. It was all anyone in rugby was talking about for at least the next week.

Ireland's *Sunday World* newspaper kicked things off when they branded the All Blacks "thugs" over O'Driscoll's tour-ending injury. The headline read: "Thugs! O'Driscoll crocked by Kiwi hoods." And by the next morning it was Woodward's turn to address the media – and make a few points of his own.

Woodward repeatedly played the television footage of the incident which showed Mealamu grabbing O'Driscoll's left leg at a ruck, and Umaga his right, and then both lifting him upwards. Another, longer-view shot, showed O'Driscoll landing on his head and neck, and Lions wing Gareth Thomas remonstrating with Australian touch judge Andy Cole. "What I heard him say clear as day was, 'leave him alone, leave him alone. The ball has gone'," Thomas said. When he then asked Cole to intervene "he said nothing, not a word".

Woodward believed the All Blacks were getting preferential treatment after what they considered to be damning evidence. He said the footage was the same two angles given to South African citing commissioner Willem Venter, who ruled Umaga and Mealamu did not have a case to answer. O'Driscoll said he was confident the tackle on him was "unnecessary and certainly beyond the rules and regulations of the game" and was dismayed Umaga had not checked on his health. "I thought it would have been a common courtesy between captains, whether he was involved or not. I'm not sure if that shows an element of guilt. That certainly disappointed me. It was one of those

moments you can see it happening, and I knew that I was in trouble from the moment I was up in the air. It was a matter of getting my head out of the way to make sure that wasn't the part of my body that took the impact. It could have been worse if I fell down on my head. I have no doubt it was some sort of spear tackle. I am absolutely gutted."

In his tour diary published at the end of 2005 O'Driscoll printed his thoughts from the days after the test. "I thought it very important to attend, to back up the anonymous words I put out in a statement last night to show clearly that it was me speaking and that I was happy to take questions on the issue. I wanted things to be transparent and in the open. I (was) determined to oppose the idea that this is a normal run-of-play rough and tumble incident. It isn't and needs to be treated differently.

"The New Zealand press put a big spin on it – special press conference called to discuss Umaga incident etc. As every single NZ journalist who has covered this tour knows full well Clive does a catch-up press conference early every Sunday morning for the Sunday papers going to bed back home. If they want to twist the facts into something different then that's up to them. But let's make sure the facts are recorded here for posterity.

"Still not a word from Tana. We played back the post-match press conference and the silence was deafening when Tana was asked about the incident and whether he was disappointed for me. He said sheepishly that there were a couple of incidents that needed looking at. That was his one comment. Graham Henry, the New Zealand coach, initially expressed ignorance of any incident involving me but said I was a good bloke and it was disappointing if my tour was over.

"The New Zealand papers are reeling off the All Black party line; that there was no foul play and that Tana Umaga had apologised at the post-match press conference. He did no such thing, as everybody knows.

He was probably told to say nothing because, as a senior member of the NZRU media team has admitted privately, they were expecting a citing and didn't want to give our QC Richard Smith any ammunition to work with.

"Apparently Umaga has been in touch with me personally to apologise. Again he has done no such thing. Somebody from the NZRU has been in touch asking for my cellphone number. As for Mealamu, his part in the incident seems to have been air-brushed from proceedings. But not by me."

His Tuesday diary entry O'Driscoll wrote: "Just received a voicemail message: 'Tana here, phone me.' Now I'm not the most comfortable at leaving voice messages myself – anybody can feel awkward and be a little abrupt – but it falls some way short of the fulsome apology and expression of concern that the New Zealand camp were proclaiming earlier today!"

The All Blacks, watching the Lions' spin on the TV news each night, were angered that their captain was being attacked. Aaron Mauger did interviews on the Tuesday after the test proclaiming Umaga's innocence telling reporters "there is no way" Umaga targeted O'Driscoll and meant to put him out of the tour.

Henry too staunchly defended his skipper. "I can't talk for him. All I will say is he's got a huge amount of respect in our camp. He's a top leader and a top professional and he's got my total backing." Henry hit out at the Lions "spin-doctors", accusing them of using the O'Driscoll incident to divert attention from their 21-3 first test defeat. He also insisted no All Black ever

went out to "maim" a rival player and he also rubbished suggestions that his players deliberately set out to cause O'Driscoll injury.

A day later it was Umaga's turn to face the media. He made it clear the injury to O'Driscoll was an accident and that the reaction to what happened was disappointing. "Especially with what we achieved on Saturday. The team should have received the accolades (for the 21-3 win) and for this to go on for so long, it is disappointing."

The most impressive sight of the day was Umaga's long-time teammate and former captain Anton Oliver flanking him during the press conference. Other senior players – Richie McCaw, Ali Williams and Chris Jack included – also fronted and made sure the media could see this united front. It was a statement that came through loud and clear – *You mess with him, you mess with us.*

Oliver told the press the All Blacks were annoyed at the "juvenile and rather transparent attempt at destabilising our team" by Woodward. He said the All Blacks were a tight group and the players were astonished what happened to O'Driscoll had become such a big issue. "It wasn't an issue at all, as far as we are concerned."

Umaga said he was a hard player but a fair one. "The way I play, I play hard. In all my games I try to play as fair as I can. That's the way I am. I really don't have much else to say other than it was an unfortunate incident and these things happen." And when quizzed by English writer, Brendan Gallagher, who was ghosting O'Driscoll's book, why he didn't check the Lions' skipper's condition when he was lying injured at Jade Stadium, Umaga said that was not his job. "I had a more important role with my team at that stage."

Even when Umaga was finally able to talk to O'Driscoll – the pair had played phone tag for four days – the Lions kept attacking the All Blacks captain. The Lions assistant coach – O'Driscoll's Ireland coach – was wheeled out to have his say. "(Tana) commiserated with

him for getting injured, as if he had naught to do with it, which I found strange," said O'Sullivan. "He hasn't apologised, which is a bit upsetting. It's a long tradition in rugby, going back to the amateur days – when an opposition player is injured, the captain always inquires after his wellbeing. So we are disappointed about that, and to say he's sorry he got hurt, without apologising, is disappointing too. Brian is still a bit upset about that, and rightly so."

Former All Blacks captain David Kirk – the only New Zealand captain to hoist the World Cup – was confident the Lions and Woodward had pushed all the wrong buttons before the second test. "What the Lions need to understand in New Zealand is that rugby is personal. The first test was personal. Attacking the All Blacks captain when you are one test down is the last thing you should do because it will only serve to galvanise New Zealand further."

Indeed. It took just 17 minutes of the second test in Wellington for Umaga to cross over for the first of the All Blacks' five tries. Carter (2), Sivivatu and McCaw got the others as the Lions were tamed 48-18.

McCaw was quick to pay tribute to his skipper. "Although we didn't focus on it a lot, we got together on Friday and said bugger it, if someone is going to have a crack at our leader we'll get round him and do our talking on the pitch and we did that. He's a superb leader and the guys were there to help him. He's a guy in the team who means heaps. We just thought let's do our speaking on the park. What happened happened and we wanted to show we're behind Tana. If anything, it brought us together tighter and made us closer as a unit."

Henry used his platform at the post-match press conference to stick up for Umaga as well. "He put up with a load of rubbish during the week from a person who doesn't know the game and doesn't have a passion for the game which was disappointing. But he showed the character he's got as a captain and a player."

That respect and loyalty towards Umaga said a massive amount about his mana within the team. And a year on from the Lions tour the media and public, when they had a chance to "go after" him, didn't. Umaga, once an easy target, was off limits. That's what happens when "great" goes before the words *All* and *Black*.

In 2006 the Hurricanes' season was marred when it was revealed that following celebrations after the Super 14 final in Christchurch 'Canes loose forward Chris Masoe punched a man in the face at a Christchurch bar – and then started crying after he was clouted on the head with a woman's handbag by Umaga.

Masoe was ridiculed for his part in the drama but Umaga escaped any negative press. And it was not good luck that saw the media and public forgive Umaga so easily. It was because of a deep respect born out of years of dedication to helping others. Forget his exploits on the rugby fields of the world – Tana Umaga, like it or not, was a role model and despite this latest transgression he was one of the good guys.

When he became an All Black for the first time in 1997 he began his "public service" by addressing Brandon Intermediate School students. He told them that when he was at school, he mucked around and never set goals for himself – "I floated in and out of school. Then I realised that I looked down on myself, and my family looked down on me."

Umaga and his Wellington captain Jason O'Halloran went to the school as part of a program to motivate students into setting goals for their future.

"Tana is a great example of what a change in mental attitude can do for you," O'Halloran said. "He was always late for practises, always the guy eating a pie in the changing rooms, the team clown. And now look at him."

The pair urged students to set little goals each week, enjoy school and strike a balance between sport and education. "And always strive to do something more – nothing is too big," Umaga told them.

A year later, after being named Wellington's Sportsman of the Year, Umaga took on a role with Save The Children NZ and actively promoted fathers spending more time with their children. He said giving time to son Cade, who was then four, was the main thing for him "especially for someone in my career. My son knows rugby means I'm away a lot, travelling. But as soon as I get back, I just spend as much time one-on-one as I can, giving him the attention that he deserves. That means just enjoying the time we are together, and doing something that he enjoys doing." That, Umaga said, was far more important and means a lot more to a child than some gift you've just picked off the shelf in a store.

Umaga was one of three rugby stars taking part in a campaign to promote fatherhood along with Northland star Norm Berryman and Crusaders legend Todd Blackadder. The campaign's catch phrase was "being a great dad is the most important position you can ever play".

"(Cade is a) normal little boy. He likes being outside, doesn't want to sit around inside. We play ball games, go for walks, go down to the playground and have a go on the swings. He likes to go on the confidence course at the playground. He'll try anything."

Umaga said it is important fathers listen to their children, "ask them about their day and listen to what they feel and how they feel. Even quite young children have feelings about things that are important to them. My partner read one particular book to Cade about a wombat. We hadn't realised the wombat was going to die in the story. Cade was quite upset; he had real deep feelings about what happened."

When he became a father Umaga said "it was just like a new feeling, it was unbelievable to have created something so beautiful. Seeing someone who is part of you like that is just awesome. You feel really proud. Being a father can be hard in the early stages, but you have to put the time into your kids all the way along, you can't just come in when they're three and begin to be a father."

Umaga embraced his ability to influence. In 1998, as a part of the Wellington Charitable Licensing Trust's Community First program he paid a memorable visit to his old school in Wainuiomata telling the teenagers he "used to drop into (school) occasionally to have lunch or go to sleep in class. I set my goals early – I was good at sport. So I didn't spend enough time in class. When I was a sixth former I was pretty much a professional – I was getting paid and I used to only come to school at lunchtime. I didn't do the work then, and now I haven't got any qualifications. So now I'm going back to school and doing a business management course. Don't put all your eggs in one basket. There's a lot in our team doing courses now. Always make sure you have a back-up plan."

"The players like doing these visits," Umaga said. "The younger kids are very receptive, but the teenagers are a bit harder." Questions included – *How much do you get paid?* Umaga deflected that one. *How long have you got your (sponsored) car for?* "Not long enough," Umaga said. "It's got to go back." *Do you like sevens?* "No mate, you have to be too fit." *Who's the fastest All Black over 10 metres?* "Jonah. He only needs two steps."

He had them eating out of his hand. There was little doubt being a father – and the joys it can bring – was something he wanted every New Zealand father to discover. In 2000 he joined forces with Jonah Lomu, *Xena: Warrior Princess* star Lucy Lawless and media maestro Paul Holmes and approached Commissioner

"The way I play, I play hard. In all my games I try to play as fair as I can. That's the way I am. I really don't have much else to say other than it was an unfortunate incident and these things happen."

for Children Roger McClay offering their help to stamp out child abuse. And he offered his name to a campaign to reduce the number of pedestrians being killed on the nation's roads. Land Transport Safety Authority figures showed Pacific Island children are seven times more likely to be injured or killed as pedestrians than other children. "I have to do something," Umaga said at the time.

A year later, in 2001, a nervous Umaga inspired teenagers to follow their dreams in his first public speech, given at the launch of Project K, a program aimed at giving youth direction through a three-week wilderness adventure, a 10-day community challenge and a 12-month mentoring program. He spoke of his upbringing in Wainuiomata, advice given by his brother and sister, and the importance of self-belief and having the confidence to follow your dreams. Others on hand at the launch were Prime Minister Helen Clark and Women's Refuge boss Merepeka Raukawa-Tait.

Then in 2002, when he was being frozen out by All Blacks coach John Mitchell, Umaga had the time to align himself with a new campaign Light on Every Bike – inspired by the death of 15-year-old Palmerston North Boys' High School student Jason Ma in a traffic accident. And at an expo taking place at the Little Theatre in Lower Hutt to encourage Pacific Island students to explore career options and develop their potential Umaga fronted up at no-charge to the organiser.

And in this world where All Blacks are expected to "hate" their opponents as they "go to war" Umaga stood alone on the field as well. When Wales No 8 Colin Charvis was knocked out in a tackle by Jerry Collins in Hamilton in 2003, Umaga rushed to his aid, turning Charvis on his side to clear his airways. It was an action that would be rewarded. In 2004 he was recognised by the International Committee of Fair Play and given the Pierre de Coubertin Trophy for Fair Play. He was the first New Zealand recipient, with past winners including Arthur Ashe, Bobby Charlton, Martina Navratilova and Sergei Bubka.

"I'm humbled and it is a great honour for me to receive this award," Umaga said. "Sport is competitive but it doesn't mean that we should turn the other way when an opposition player is injured. If a similar incident happens in the future, I won't hesitate to help out."

Two years later Umaga was asked by Wainuiomata High School principal Rob Mill to talk to school children about an anti-bullying scheme which he had been developing for three months. Umaga fronted and revealed he was bullied as a youngster. It did not last long, but he did not handle it the best way. "I didn't tell anyone. I was a bit ashamed of it. If I knew then what I know now, it would have been different." He remembered when, as a young player trying to break into the All Blacks, he went to sit at a breakfast table with some of the senior players. "They were talking about investing in the sharemarket… about maybe investing $1000, and they asked me if I invested. I said, 'A thousand bucks! No, I just save my money.' They laughed… made me feel small. I got up and joined the younger guys at another table."

And then in February 2005 the Labour government asked him to front a $16 million campaign to encourage parents to get involved in their children's education. Education Ministry officials signed him up after he expressed interest in supporting an education cause. At the project launch at Wellington's Lyall Bay School Umaga said he tried to spend time with his children, ask about their day and take an interest in what they were doing.

"Parents as first teachers is something I firmly

believe in… I have an 11-year-old son who has just started a new school. I come home from training a bit tired. I am forcing myself to get up and help him with his homework. I have my first meeting with my son's teacher next week. I will try to attend that, which will be the first one in a while."

While he was on tour with the All Blacks in 2005 he took time out in between the Irish and English test to play a key role at the NZRU's successful World Cup 2011 hosting bid in front of the International Rugby Board bosses. Umaga joined the Prime Minister and NZRU CEO Chris Moller and chairman Jock Hobbs in the presentation group and won praise from the nation's leader. Sports Minister Trevor Mallard reported that Clark thought the team presentation to the rugby board was magnificent. "She singled out Tana as speaking from the heart, without notes and without missing a beat, as being one of the most special presentations she has ever seen."

Umaga reminded the IRB that a World Cup was not just about dollars, but also about the players. He told them that the players would enjoy a World Cup in New Zealand and doffed his hat to his Samoan heritage when he said it would be a tournament for the Pacific Islands to embrace, too.

Indeed it was as much about the man as the rugby when the French club Toulon agreed to pay him $1.4 million for eight to 10 games in the French second division in November and December 2006. "With Umaga you get the best – the best player and the best man," Toulon's president Mourad Boudjellal said.

His service on and off the field was recognised by the government in 2006 when Umaga was made an Officer of the New Zealand Order of Merit for his services to rugby. He described the experience as humbling. "When you hear about what I have done, and what everyone else has done, you start wondering about what you're doing there. Being brought up to be humble, when you hear people talking about what you've done in your life, it's a little bit embarrassing.

But it's something to be proud of. You've got to be proud of your achievements. It's great to have my parents here and my wife here. It's more for them, being able to give something back to them."

Umaga was someone putting something back into the country that had given him his opportunity to give his young family a standard of living that he never had growing up in Wainuiomata. And, as a result, the country, like his teammates, took him into their hearts.

It was why, when Umaga led the All Blacks out onto Eden Park for the third and final test against the Lions in 2005, he received the biggest cheer of all. The series had already been won but the rugby nation wanted the clean sweep. Carter, Mauger and McCaw were all out injured. Umaga moved into second-five where he could baby sit Luke McAlister in his first All Blacks start at No 10. And to rub salt into the wounds of Woodward and his Lions, Umaga grabbed two more tries in the 38-19 rout.

As the dust settled on the tour Woodward would eventually admit that he "wasn't himself" on the trip and made mistakes. He accepted that he got "fundamental things wrong" admitting: "I just wasn't myself. I was so conscious of trying to keep everyone happy and not cause any problems. One of the Ireland players had a word with me one day and said: 'We're just all disappointed – you're trying to be too diplomatic.' I regret not being myself. I didn't know the players well enough, I wasn't making the tough calls. I tried to be too clever and too diplomatic. I got some fundamental things wrong and all I can do is apologise. I've got to live with that."

He again criticised the All Blacks' stance on the O'Driscoll incident as he maintained that the two All Blacks involved should at least have been cited for the spear tackle which left the Lions and Ireland captain nursing a dislocated shoulder. "The O'Driscoll incident was massive – in no way was that just one of those things. To see them not even cite the players involved – it just wasn't right."

To his credit though before heading back to Ireland O'Driscoll told the British media that he had made his peace with Umaga. "Once I had an apology of sorts from Tana and I had spoken to him, as far as I was concerned the matter was cleared up," he said. "I would still go out and have a drink with him after a game and just carry on as normal. I still respect him hugely as a rugby player. I think what goes on on the pitch is very separate to how you carry on off it."

NOW it was the beginning of the end. Tana Umaga had four months left as an All Black. He knew it. His wife knew it. His manager knew it. And Graham Henry knew it.

All that separated Umaga from All Blacks rugby and international retirement was two tests against Australia and South Africa and a Grand Slam at the end of the year against Wales, Ireland, England and Scotland.

After the highs of the Lions tour the biggest obstacle to Tri-nations and Bledisloe Cup success was complacency. And if they were after a wake-up call it came in the tournament's opening game against the defending champions in Cape Town. The game was lost 22-16 and added to the misery was Umaga limping off the field with ankle ligament damage.

But Umaga was determined to be fit for the game against the Wallabies in Sydney in seven days. "It's the Bledisloe Cup; need you say more?" Umaga told the *Dominion* when asked if he would front. "We worked so hard to get it back, now we have to work even harder to keep it. It's up to us who did get it back to keep pushing that across to the young guys who weren't there. We have to instill in them the history of the Bledisloe Cup and what it means to us."

Privately Umaga knew that if the Cup was lost, he'd never get the chance to win it back. But that didn't matter with the All Blacks – with Umaga in the No 13 jersey – convincingly winning 30-13.

Wins against the Boks (31-27) and Wallabies (34-24) followed in Dunedin and Auckland and the

Tri-nations trophy was on its way back to the NZRU's HQ in Wellington.

Now the last part of Umaga's glory year was to be played out. He led a team which had every chance of becoming only the second All Blacks side to complete a Grand Slam. It was the first time the All Blacks had been able to go for it since Graham Mourie's side managed it in 1978. It was New Zealand's seventh attempt at the landmark since the Originals first toured in 1905.

In contrast South Africa have landed four Grand Slams in eight attempts, while Australia have one success (1984) from seven.

New Zealand lost to Wales on that very first trip while Cliff Porter's Invincibles of 1924–25 did not play Scotland because of an argument over match-fees. The 1935–36 All Blacks fell to Wales (13-12) and England (13-0) while the 1953–54 tourists were beaten 13-8 by Wales, the last Welsh success against New Zealand. Scotland blotted Wilson Whineray's copybook 10 years later, drawing 0-0 at Murrayfield – the last scoreless draw in an international match. Ireland also drew, 10-10 with Ian Kirkpatrick's All Blacks in 1972–73.

But it was the 1967 All Blacks side coached by Fred Allen who are considered to be one of the finest touring sides. Led by Brian Lochore, they swept through Britain unbeaten, drawing only with East Wales in Cardiff. They beat England (23-11), Wales (13-6) and Scotland (14-3), despite the sending-off of Colin Meads. But the outbreak of foot-and-mouth disease in 1967 prevented New Zealand from fulfilling fixtures in Ireland.

The toughest for the 2005 side was always going to be the third match – against England at Twickenham. The test with the most interest was always going to be the second match – against Ireland in Dublin where Umaga would come face-to-face with Brian O'Driscoll's countrymen.

First up though was a Welsh side missing a number of their front line stars. It was expected to be a formality and it was – the All Blacks cruising to a 41-3 victory before heading to Ireland.

Umaga, speaking at a luncheon in September 2006, said he spent the majority of his time in Dublin hunkered down in his hotel room after the *Sunday Mirror* printed a story suggesting death threats had been made against the New Zealand captain. And rather than feed Umaga to the lions at Lansdowne Road, Henry opted to rest his skipper for the test and at the same time give captain-in-waiting Richie McCaw another test in charge.

He returned for the Twickenham test and as if on cue, scored a try to help set up a gritty 23-19 win. Now, all that stood between Umaga and his retirement, and the team and a Grand Slam was Scotland.

The famed TVNZ commentator Keith Quinn was the first to publicly float news that Umaga would retire after the last test of the tour. Umaga's manager Rob Brady fielded calls on a daily basis for two months before the tour enquiring about Umaga's status. Brady denied the story and it wasn't until the *New Zealand Herald*'s front page story by Wynne Gray on the morning of the Scotland test when it was accepted to be true. Umaga would wait until January to officially announce the decision but it was clear to everyone that Murrayfield would be his 74th and last test for the All Blacks.

Umaga told his teammates after the 29-10 win that rugby with Wellington and the Hurricanes would become his focus. Umaga opted against taking up a clause in his contract that allowed the opportunity to take a temporary break from the All Blacks. All other contracted players must be available for international selection, but Umaga's longevity and close family granted him an exemption. "I got pretty choked up and I think I shocked a few people in the room, too," Umaga said. His decision to spend more time with wife Rochelle and children Cade, 12, Gabrielle, five, Lily-Kate, 16 months and Anise, born in September 2006, ended one of the All Blacks' most popular captaincies.

"My reason for retiring is that I want to spend more time with my family," he said. "I sacrificed a lot of time with my family to wear the jersey. Now it's time to sacrifice something for my family. My kids are older now and I want to play a major part in their lives as they grow up. I just wanted to play in the All Black jersey. Winning was great, but when I look back and show the kids the team photos and say, 'Mate, that's me; I wore that', it's those things that really count, not winning the World Cup."

The tributes flowed in…

Henry said Umaga was one of the greats. "He was very brave, led from the front, fine defender, huge determination to win. He's one of the great All Black captains."

Leon MacDonald, the All Black fullback who filled his centre role when Umaga was injured at the 2003 World Cup said the All Blacks environment wouldn't be the same without T. "He's been a part of the All Blacks for years and you think guys like that will always be around. It will certainly be bit different without him in the team. I've been a fan of his from when I was a teenager and still playing for Marlborough. He's an easy going guy, he's relaxed and enjoys his rugby. He gets on well with all the guys and connects well with new players coming into the team. It's a sign of a good captain that he can relate to all players, the young ones and those who've played 50 tests."

All Blacks assistant coach Wayne Smith – who pushed Umaga towards a leadership role when he had charge of the All Blacks in 2000 and 2001 – shared a close bond with Umaga. He said Umaga's character and mana stood out even more than a playing ability that had been proven many times over. "There are good players around who are going to be good All Blacks but we're losing a unique one. To replace Tana as a player probably can't be done. If you could retire a jersey, I think his would be retired."

Justin Marshall – a former All Blacks captain himself – agreed with Smith's interpretation. "Tana was

unique," the 81 test veteran said. "He's an inspirational captain. He was different from the captains I was used to in the All Blacks. Tana is not a talker, he doesn't speak a lot, but when he does speak he is someone to listen to. He is not a ranting, raving captain who sits a team down and talks tactics to them. He's a doer, he leads by example. He does things that he wants people to be doing and that gets people to follow. It goes to show that you don't have to follow by someone telling you what to do, you just get out there and do the same."

Zinzan Brooke – who wanted Umaga axed in 2004 – was full of praise. "What Tana Umaga has achieved in the last couple of years means he deserves to be held up there with the great All Blacks captains. He has been the father figure of the team and very instrumental in making them the side they are today. Tana was starting out with the All Blacks just as I was finishing my Test career in 1997. He was a great player at an early age but I didn't see the captaincy credentials then. He was one of those at the front of the bus, very quiet, but it was great to have him around. He was absolute dynamite, like another Jonah (Lomu). He was a great player and a very natural winger. I'd have put him ahead of guys like Doug Howlett and Joe Rokocoko in the current All Blacks team. When he slowed down a bit he made a successful transition to centre, and what he has done in helping the rest of the team has been crucial. He has played a huge part in giving them that self-belief, and has a great rapport with the players with Pacific Island heritage like himself. A lot of them are shy and quiet and need an arm around them, and it takes a certain person to push the right buttons. It is important someone else carries that mantle now, and the captaincy will find the right person. There are certain players that it sits happily on their shoulders, and there are others like Taine Randell, with whom I never thought it did. The All Blacks captain needs to have the respect that Tana has."

And Todd Blackadder – another of Umaga's former captains was just as glowing. "I remember Tana playing

"I just needed to get away from the game a little bit. It's as mental as it is physical really. Having the captaincy with the All Blacks was great, but I took the losses hard. I took them personally and it took me a while to put them behind me. I had to mourn those losses because it really did affect me and obviously my performance in that last game was not up to my standards."

for me as captain and what I liked about him then, and still do now, is that he is just himself all the time; he never understates or exaggerates anything," Blackadder said. "I thought he dealt with the whole O'Driscoll affair very well. Yes, it was dangerous what he did, but I know Tana and it would never have been deliberate. But I think he is going out at the right time. He's been a great player and one of the very best All Blacks. He has been a key part of providing the launch pad that New Zealand rugby has needed to bring on the next generation and if they do go on and win the next World Cup there will be a debt of gratitude owed to Tana."

Perhaps the most touching tribute came from Wayne Smith who revealed Umaga – after telling his teammates of his retirement in the changing sheds at Murrayfield – then received a rare tribute from his teammates… "The players cried when he told them. That's a huge mark of respect not afforded to many players. When I retired they cheered, for him they cried."

THERE is a satisfying ordinariness about Umaga, as if to confirm the happenstance of success. As if to say; *He's no more groomed for fame than you.* Which is really to say, since the education of a private school or having the childhood rearing that a rugged New Zealand farm offers is no longer a prerequisite of success in rugby, you could be an All Black too.

Probably, of course, you couldn't, or there would be 4.2 million players for Graham Henry to select from. But watching Tana Umaga operate, looking rumpled and a little disorganised, he offered hope… for a moment at least.

Perception, of course, is a powerful thing. From the outer circle he seems indifferent, almost aloof. He smiles a lot. That suggests a certain relaxed state of mind. There's plenty to worry about but that would be a waste of time. He's got other things on his mind.

"The future," he said. "That's what counts. I guess you could say I have a history… a record. But it's kinda funny actually 'cause the only people that care about it are people that aren't in my life."

Perception, of course, is often wrong. Tana Umaga is disciplined. Tana Umaga is focused. Tana Umaga is a leader. Indeed, all of a sudden, Tana Umaga was everything we have ever wanted our All Blacks to be.

TANA: THE ALL BLACK

FULL NAME	Jonathan Falefasa Umaga
BORN	Sunday, 27 May 1973 in Lower Hutt
AGE	33
PHYSICAL	1.87m, 101kg
POSITION	Centre
LAST SCHOOL	Parkway College
RUGBY CLUB	
(First made All Blacks from)	Petone
PROVINCE	Wellington
SUPER 14 TEAM	Hurricanes
RUGBY NICKNAME	T
ALL BLACK DEBUT	Saturday, 14 June 1997
	v Fiji at Albany
	aged 24 years, 18 days
INTERNATIONAL DEBUT	Saturday, 14 June 1997
	v Fiji at Albany
	aged 24 years, 18 days
LAST TEST	Saturday, 26 November 2005
	v Scotland at Edinburgh
	aged 32 years, 183 days
ALL BLACK TESTS	74 (21 as Captain)
ALL BLACK GAMES	5 (0 as Captain)
TOTAL ALL BLACK MATCHES	79 (21 as Captain)
ALL BLACK TEST POINTS	180pts (36t, 0c, 0p, 0dg)
ALL BLACK GAME POINTS	5pts (1t, 0c, 0p, 0dg)
TOTAL ALL BLACK POINTS	185pts (37t, 0c, 0p, 0dg)
ALL BLACK NUMBER	961

1997

14 Jun	vs **Fiji** at Albany 71-5
21 Jun	vs **Argentina** at Wellington 93-8
28 Jun	vs **Argentina** at Hamilton 62-10
5 Jul	vs **Australia** at Christchurch 30-13 (-)
19 Jul	vs **South Africa** at Johannesburg 35-32 (-)
9 Aug	vs **South Africa** at Auckland 55-35
11 Nov	vs Wales 'A' at Pontypridd 51-8
18 Nov	vs Emerging England at Huddersfield 59-22 (-)
25 Nov	vs English Rugby Partnership XV at Bristol 18-11
2 Dec	vs England 'A' at Leicester 30-19

1999

11 Jun	vs New Zealand 'A' at Christchurch 22-11 (-)
18 Jun	vs **Samoa** at Albany 71-13
26 Jun	vs **France** at Wellington 54-7
10 Jul	vs **South Africa** at Dunedin 28-0 (-)
24 Jul	vs **Australia** at Auckland 34-15 (-)
7 Aug	vs **South Africa** at Pretoria 34-18 (-)
28 Aug	vs **Australia** at Sydney 7-28
3 Oct	vs **Tonga** at Bristol 45-9
9 Oct	vs **England** at London 30-16
24 Oct	vs **Scotland** at Edinburgh 30-18 (-)
31 Oct	vs **France** at London 31-43
4 Nov	vs **South Africa** at Cardiff 18-22 (-)

2000

16 Jun	vs **Tonga** at Albany 102-0
24 Jun	vs **Scotland** at Dunedin 69-20
1 Jul	vs **Scotland** at Auckland 48-14 (-)
15 Jul	vs **Australia** at Sydney 39-35
22 Jul	vs **South Africa** at Christchurch 25-12
5 Aug	vs **Australia** at Wellington 23-24
19 Aug	vs **South Africa** at Johannesburg 40-46
11 Nov	vs **France** at Paris 39-26
18 Nov	vs **France** at Marseille 33-42
25 Nov	vs **Italy** at Genova 56-19

2001

16 Jun   vs **Samoa** at Albany 50-6
23 Jun   vs **Argentina** at Christchurch 67-19
30 Jun   vs **France** at Wellington 37-12
21 Jul   vs **South Africa** at Cape Town 12-3
11 Aug vs **Australia** at Dunedin 15-23
25 Aug vs **South Africa** at Auckland 26-15
1 Sep   vs **Australia** at Sydney 26-29
17 Nov vs **Ireland** at Dublin 40-29
24 Nov vs **Scotland** at Edinburgh 37-6
1 Dec   vs **Argentina** at Buenos Aires 24-20

2002

15 Jun   vs **Ireland** at Dunedin 15-6 (-)
29 Jun   vs **Fiji** at Wellington 68-18 (-)
20 Jul   vs **South Africa** at Wellington 41-20 (+)
3 Aug   vs **Australia** at Sydney 14-16
10 Aug vs **South Africa** at Durban 30-23
9 Nov   vs **England** at London 28-31
16 Nov vs **France** at Paris 20-20
23 Nov vs **Wales** at Cardiff 43-17

2003

14 Jun   vs **England** at Wellington 13-15
21 Jun   vs **Wales** at Hamilton 55-3
28 Jun   vs **France** at Christchurch 31-23
19 Jul   vs **South Africa** at Pretoria 52-16
26 Jul   vs **Australia** at Sydney 50-21
9 Aug   vs **South Africa** at Dunedin 19-11
16 Aug vs **Australia** at Auckland 21-17
11 Oct   vs **Italy** at Melbourne 70-7 (-)

2004

12 Jun   vs **England** at Dunedin 36-3 (Captain)
19 Jun   vs **England** at Auckland 36-12 (Captain)
26 Jun   vs **Argentina** at Hamilton 41-7 (Captain)
10 Jul   vs **Pacific Islanders** at Albany 41-26 (Captain)
17 Jul   vs **Australia** at Wellington 16-7 (Captain)
24 Jul   vs **South Africa** at Christchurch 23-21 (Captain)
7 Aug   vs **Australia** at Sydney 18-23 (Captain)
14 Aug   vs **South Africa** at Johannesburg 26-40 (Captain)
13 Nov   vs **Italy** at Rome 59-10 (-) (Captain)
27 Nov   vs **France** at Paris 45-6 (Captain)

2005

10 Jun   vs **Fiji** at Albany 91-0 (-) (Captain)
25 Jun   vs **British and Irish Lions** at Christchurch 21-3 (-) (Captain)
2 Jul   vs **British and Irish Lions** at Wellington 48-18 (Captain)
9 Jul   vs **British and Irish Lions** at Auckland 38-19 (Captain)
6 Aug   vs **South Africa** at Capetown 16-22 (-) (Captain)
13 Aug   vs **Australia** at Sydney 30-13 (Captain)
27 Aug   vs **South Africa** at Dunedin 31-27 (Captain)
3 Sep   vs **Australia** at Auckland 34-24 (Captain)
5 Nov   vs **Wales** at Cardiff 41-3 (Captain)
19 Nov   vs **England** at London 23-19 (Captain)
26 Nov   vs **Scotland** at Edinburgh 29-10 (Captain)

* statistics courtesy of the New Zealand Rugby Museum

(+) = substitute
(-) = replaced

TEST RECORD BY NATION

	P	W	D	L	t	c	p	dg	pts
Argentina	5	5	-	-	5	-	-	-	25
Australia	14	8	-	6	2	-	-	-	10
British and Irish Lions	3	3	-	-	3	-	-	-	15
England	6	4	-	2	1	-	-	-	5
Fiji	3	3	-	-	3	-	-	-	15
France	8	5	1	2	4	-	-	-	20
Ireland	2	2	-	-	-	-	-	-	-
Italy	3	3	-	-	2	-	-	-	10
Pacific Islanders	1	1	-	-	1	-	-	-	5
Samoa	2	2	-	-	2	-	-	-	10
Scotland	5	5	-	-	7	-	-	-	35
South Africa	17	13	-	4	3	-	-	-	15
Tonga	2	2	-	-	2	-	-	-	10
Wales	3	3	-	-	1	-	-	-	5
TOTALS	74	59	1	14	36	0	0	0	180

ABOUT THE AUTHOR

This is John Matheson's seventh book. In 1999 he collaborated with Eric Rush on the best seller *Gold Rush* and in 2000 he penned the critically acclaimed *Black Days* – a series of interviews with rugby superstars recounting their experiences of playing against the All Blacks. In 2002 there was another No 1 best seller – *Rushie*, the second book with Rush and a biography on league star Stacey Jones. They were followed by *Life on the Run* the best selling biography on All Blacks great Christian Cullen – the third biggest selling rugby book in New Zealand. In 2004 he completed the Rush trilogy when he wrote, *Adrenalin Rush*.

Throughout his 20 years in journalism he has worked in Auckland, Christchurch, London and San Diego and has covered such diverse sporting events as the Rugby World Cup, Grand Slam tennis, World Cup soccer, the NBA and the America's Cup. While in New Zealand he has worked for the *Auckland Star* and *Sunday Star*, contributed to the *New Zealand Herald* and the *Dominion*, and is still the longest serving editor of *NZ Rugby World*. He is currently an Assistant Editor and Sports Editor at *Sunday News*.

Matheson – a five-time recipient at the Qantas Media Awards – directed the Sky TV rugby show *Offside* and lists completing the Ironman, playing for and coaching Auckland basketball teams and being offered a trial by Harry Redknapp at Bournemouth as his proudest achievements. He wishes to thank Celebrity Books' Bill Honeybone for his guidance and support. And he dedicates this book to Jessica May Galu and their guiding light, daughter Ava-Dawn May Matheson.

ISBN 1-877252-29-8

Published in 2006 by Celebrity Books
Private Box 302 750
North Harbour, Auckland
New Zealand

©2006 John Matheson
The moral rights of the author have been asserted

Cover design: Dexter Fry
Book design and production: Gina Hochstein
Printed in China by Prolong Press Ltd, Hong Kong

10 9 8 7 6 5 4 3 2 1

Celebrity Books is the imprint of The Celebrity Book Company Limited.
Level 1, 19 Tarndale Grove
Albany, North Shore City
New Zealand

PHOTOGRAPHS

Jo Caird: pages 2, 11, 15, 16, 22, 25, 26, 29, 30, 31, 32, 34, 39, 40, 41, 44, 46, 51, 52, 53, 55, 56, 59, 60, 63, 64, 65, 67, 69, 70, 72, 75, 76, 78, 79, 80, 83, 101, 105, 108, 110, 113, 121, 127, 135, 136, 140
Tranz/Corbis: pages 4, 92, 106, 114, 118, 125
Tranz/Rex Features: pages 84, 93, 94, 96, 102, 117, 128, 131, 132, 142, 147, 148, 152
Lawrence Smith, Fairfax: pages 6, 9, 10, 12, 18, 21, 37, 43, 48, 86, 89, 91, 99, 122, 123, 138

"My reason for retiring is that I want to spend more time with my family. I sacrificed a lot of time with my family to wear the jersey. Now it's time to sacrifice something for my family. My kids are older now and I want to play a major part in their lives as they grow up. I just wanted to play in the All Black jersey. Winning was great, but when I look back and show the kids the team photos and say, 'Mate, that's me; I wore that', it's those things that really count, not winning the World Cup."